Cisco Networking Academy Program: Engineering Journal and Workbook, Volume II
Second Edition

Cisco Systems, Inc.

Cisco Networking Academy Program

Cisco Press

Cisco Press
201 West 103rd Street
Indianapolis, Indiana 46290 USA

Cisco Networking Academy Program:
Engineering Journal and Workbook, Volume II
Second Edition

Cisco Systems, Inc.

Cisco Networking Academy Program

Published by:
Cisco Press
201 West 103rd Street
Indianapolis, IN 46290 USA

Printed in the United States of America   3 4 5 6 7 8 9 0

ISBN: 1-58713-031-9

Trademark Acknowledgments

Warning and Disclaimer

Feedback Information

At Cisco Press, our goal is to create in-depth technical books of the highest quality and value. Each book is crafted with care and precision, undergoing rigorous development that involves the unique expertise of members from the professional technical community.

Readers' feedback is a natural continuation of this process. If you have any comments regarding how we could improve the quality of this book, or otherwise alter it to better suit your needs, you can contact us at feedback@ciscopress.com. Please make sure to include the book title and ISBN in your message.

We greatly appreciate your assistance.

Publisher	*John Wait*
Executive Editor	*Carl Lindholm*
Cisco Systems Program Manager	*Bob Anstey*
Managing Editor	*Patrick Kanouse*
Senior Project Editor	*Sheri Replin*
Product Manager	*Shannon Gross*

Table of Contents

Preface

Since 1997, the Cisco Networking Academy Program has instituted an e-learning model that integrates the multimedia delivery of a networking curriculum with testing, performance-based skills assessment, evaluation, and reporting through a Web interface. The Cisco Networking Academy curriculum goes beyond traditional computer-based instruction by helping students develop practical networking knowledge and skills in a hands-on environment. In a lab setting that closely corresponds to a real networking environment, students work with the architecture and infrastructure pieces of networking technology. As a result, students learn the principles and practices of networking technology.

The Cisco Networking Academy Program provides in-depth and meaningful networking content, which is being used by Regional and Local Academies to teach students around the world by utilizing the curriculum to integrate networking instruction into the classroom. The focus of the Networking Academy program is on the integration of a Web-based network curriculum into the learning environment. This element is addressed through intensive staff development for instructors and innovative classroom materials and approaches to instruction, which are provided by Cisco. The participating educators are provided with resources, the means of remote access to online support, and the knowledge base for the effective classroom integration of the Cisco Networking Academy curriculum into the classroom learning environment. As a result, the Networking Academy program provides the means for the dynamic exchange of information by providing a suite of services that redefine the way instructional resources are disseminated, resulting in a many-to-many interactive and collaborative network of teachers and students functioning to meet diverse educational needs.

The Networking Academy curriculum is especially exciting to educators and students because the courseware is interactive. Because of the growing use of interactive technologies, the curriculum is an exciting new way to convey instruction with new interactive technologies that allow instructors and trainers to mix a number of media, including audio, video, text, numerical data, and graphics. Consequently, students can select different media from the computer screen and tweak their instructional content to meet their instructional needs, and educators have the option of either designing their own environment for assessment or selecting from the applicable assessments.

Finally, by developing a curriculum that recognizes the changing classroom and workforce demographics, the globalization of the economy, changing workforce knowledge and skill requirements, and the role of technology in education, the Cisco Networking Academy Program supports national educational goals for K-12 education. As support for the Networking Academy program, Cisco Press published this book, *Cisco Networking Academy Program: Engineering Journal and Workbook*, Volume II, Second Edition, as a further complement to the curriculum used in the Cisco Networking Academy Program.

Introduction

Cisco Networking Academy Program: Engineering Journal and Workbook, Volume II, Second Edition, acts as a supplement to your classroom and laboratory experience with the Cisco Networking Academy Program, whose curriculum is designed to empower you to enter employment or further education and training in the computer networking field.

This tool is designed to further train you beyond the online training materials that you have already used in this program, along with the topics pertaining to the Cisco Certified Network Associate (CCNA) exam. This book closely follows the style and format that Cisco has incorporated into the curriculum. In addition, this book follows the two-semester curriculum model that has already been developed for the Cisco Networking Academy Program. The *Engineering Journal and Workbook* provides you with additional exercises and activities that reinforces your learning. We also included writing opportunities that help you learn to establish and keep an engineering journal. We recommend that you keep a technical, or engineering, journal. Typically, a journal is a paper-bound composition book in which pages are not added or subtracted, but dated. The types of journal entries most applicable for Networking Academy students include daily reflections, troubleshooting details, lab procedures and observations, equipment logs, hardware and software notes, and router configurations. The journal becomes more important as you do more network design and installation work, so good habits can be developed by starting a journal the first day of Semester 1. In this book, you are asked to keep your journal on a daily basis.

The Washington Project

In Chapter 4, you are introduced to the Washington Project. This project helps you learn by applying the knowledge that you gain to a real-life example. The Washington Project is a performance assessment that is introduced in the first semester of the curriculum. However, the actual project work is not done until Semesters 3 and 4 of the curriculum, which are covered in this workbook. Each chapter contains content, concepts, and topics that help you build the knowledge you need to complete the Washington Project. Design information regarding this project is in Appendix B, "Washington Project Background."

Chapter 1   Review: The OSI Reference Model and Routing

Introduction

Networks are complex environments that involve multiple media, multiple protocols, and interconnections to networks outside an organization's central office. Well-designed and carefully installed networks can reduce the problems associated with growth as a networking environment evolves.

Designing, building, and maintaining a network can be a challenging task. Even a small network that consists of only 50 nodes can pose complex problems that lead to unpredictable results. Large networks that feature thousands of nodes can pose even more complex problems. Despite improvements in equipment performance and media capabilities, designing and building a network is difficult.

This chapter reviews the Open System Interconnection (OSI) reference model and overviews network planning and design considerations related to routing. Much of this information should be familiar because you were introduced to these concepts in the first year of the Cisco Networking Academy Program. Using the OSI reference model as a reference for network design can facilitate changes. Using the OSI reference model as a hierarchical structure for network design allows you to design networks in layers. The OSI reference model is at the heart of building and designing networks, with every layer performing a specific task in order to promote data communications. In the world of networking, Layers 1 through 4 are the focus. These four layers define the following:

- The type and speed of LAN and WAN media to be implemented
- How data is sent across the media
- The type of addressing schemes used
- How data is reliably sent across the network and how flow control is accomplished
- The type of routing protocol implemented

Concept Questions

Demonstrate your knowledge of these concepts by answering the following questions in the space provided.

- By using layers, the OSI model simplifies the task required for two computers to communicate. **Can you explain why?**

- Each layer's protocol exchanges information, called PDUs, between peer layers. **Can you explain how this is done?**

- Each layer depends on the service function of the OSI reference model layer below it. The lower layer uses encapsulation to put the PDU from the upper layer into its data field; then it can add whatever headers and trailers the layer will use to perform its function. **Can you explain the concept of encapsulation?**

- The term *Ethernet* is often used to refer to all CSMA/CD LANs that generally conform to Ethernet specifications, including IEEE 802.3.The Ethernet and 802.3 data links provide data transport across the physical link joining two devices. **Can you explain what the term Ethernet means?**

- IP provides connectionless, best-effort delivery routing of datagrams. It is not concerned with the content of the datagrams, but it looks for a way to move the datagrams to their destination. **What is a datagram?**

- ARP is used to map a known IP address to a MAC sublayer address to allow communication on a multiaccess medium such as Ethernet. **What is ARP and how does it work?**

- Most routing protocols can be classified into one of two basic protocols: distance vector or link state. **What are the differences between the two types of protocols?**

- Examples of IP routing protocols include RIP, IGRP, OSPF, and EIGRP. **Explain the differences between these different types of protocols.**

Engineering Journal
In the space provided, answer the Concept Questions.

Vocabulary Exercise Chapter 1   Name: _____

Date: _____   Class: _____

Define the following terms as completely as you can. Use the online Chapter 1 or the *Cisco Networking Academy Program: Second-Year Companion Guide*, Second Edition, material for help.

Application layer

_____
_____

ARP (Address Resolution Protocol)

_____
_____

Cisco IOS (Internetwork Operating System) software

_____
_____

Data link layer

_____
_____

Datagram

_____
_____

Default route

_____
_____

Distance-vector routing protocol

_____
_____

Dynamic routing

_____
_____

EIGRP (Enhanced Interior Gateway Routing Protocol)

_____

_____

Flow control

_____

_____

ICMP (Internet Control Message Protocol)

_____

_____

IGRP (Interior Gateway Routing Protocol)

_____

_____

IP address

_____

_____

MAC (Media Access Control)

_____

_____

Network

_____

_____

Network layer

_____

_____

NIC (network interface card)

_____

_____

Packet

_____

_____

Focus Questions   **Name:** _____

Date: _____   **Class:** _____

1. List each of the layers of the OSI model and identify their function. Indicate what networking and internetworking devices operate at each of the layers. Be specific.

2. Define the following terms:

SPF (shortest path first) protocol

_____

_____

Static routing

_____

_____

Stub network

_____

_____

Presentation

_____

_____

RARP (Reverse Address Resolution Protocol)

_____

_____

3. Outline a presentation that you might give to your parents that explains the OSI model. What examples might you use to do this?

_____

_____

_____

_____

_____

_____

_____

_____

_____

_____

_____

_____

_____

_____

_____

_____

_____

_____

_____

_____

_____

_____

_____

_____

CCNA Review

The following questions help you review for the CCNA exam. Answers to these questions are found in Appendix C, "Answers to the CCNA Exam Review Questions."

1. Which OSI layer supports a file transfer capability?
   a. Application layer
   b. Network layer
   c. Presentation layer
   d. Session layer
   e. Physical layer

2. What OSI layer negotiates data transfer syntax such as ASCII?
   a. Network layer
   b. Transport layer
   c. Application layer
   d. Physical layer
   e. Presentation layer

3. Which OSI layer deals with session and connection coordination?
   a. Physical layer
   b. Data link layer
   c. Transport layer
   d. Session layer
   e. Presentation layer

4. What OSI layer supports reliable connections for data transport services?
   a. Application layer
   b. Session layer
   c. Presentation layer
   d. Physical layer
   e. Transport layer

5. At what layer does routing occur?
   a. Session layer
   b. Application layer
   c. Network layer
   d. Transport layer
   e. Data link layer

Engineering Journal (Continued)

Chapter 2   LAN Switching

Introduction

Today, network designers are moving away from using bridges and hubs to primarily using switches and routers to build networks. Chapter 1, "Review: The OSI Reference Model and Routing," provided a review of the OSI reference model and an overview of network planning and design considerations related to routing.

This chapter discusses problems in a local-area network (LAN) and possible solutions that can improve LAN performance. You learn about LAN congestion, its effect on network performance, and the advantages of LAN segmentation in a network. In addition, you learn about the advantages and disadvantages of using bridges, switches, and routers for LAN segmentation and the effects of switching, bridging, and routing on network throughput. Finally, you learn about Ethernet, Fast Ethernet, and VLANs and the benefits of these technologies.

Concept Questions

Demonstrate your knowledge of these concepts by answering the following questions in the space provided.

- The combination of more powerful computers/workstations and network-intensive applications has created a need for bandwidth that is much greater than the 10 Mbps available on shared Ethernet/802.3 LANs. **What technology offers a solution to this bandwidth problem?**
- As more people utilize a network to share large files, access file servers, and connect to the Internet, network congestion occurs. **What is network congestion and what effect does it have on the network?**
- A network can be divided in smaller units, called segments. Each segment is considered its own collision domain. **Does this reduce network congestion? Explain.**
- A LAN that uses a switched Ethernet topology creates a network that behaves like it only has two nodes—the sending node and the receiving node. **Why is this so?**
- Switches achieve high-speed transfer by reading the destination Layer 2 MAC address of the packet, much the way a bridge does. This leads to a high rate of speed for packet forwarding. **How does a switch differ from a bridge?**
- Ethernet switching increases the bandwidth available on a network. **Exactly how does this occur? What is Gigabit Ethernet?**
- Symmetric switching is one way of characterizing a LAN switch according to the bandwidth allocated to each port on the switch. **Are there other ways of characterizing a LAN Switch?**
- An asymmetric LAN switch provides switched connections between ports of unlike bandwidth, such as a combination of 10-Mbps and 100-Mbps ports. **What are the differences between symmetric and asymmetric switching? Can you draw a schematic of each?**

- The main function of the Spanning-Tree Protocol is to allow duplicate switched/bridged paths without suffering the latency effects of loops in the network. **What does this mean to a network manager and why is it important?**

Engineering Journal
In the space provided, answer the Concept Questions.

_____
_____
_____
_____
_____
_____
_____
_____
_____
_____
_____
_____
_____
_____
_____
_____
_____
_____
_____
_____
_____
_____
_____
_____
_____
_____
_____
_____
_____
_____
_____

Vocabulary Exercise Chapter 2   Name: _____

Date: _____   Class: _____

Define the following terms as completely as you can. Use the online Chapter 2 or the *Cisco Networking Academy Program: Second-Year Companion Guide*, Second Edition, material for help.

Acknowledgment

_____
_____

Backbone

_____
_____

Bandwidth

_____
_____

Broadcast

_____
_____

Collision domain

_____
_____

Congestion

_____
_____

Cut-through

_____
_____

Fast Ethernet

_____
_____

Fast-forward switching

_____

_____

Fragment-free switching

_____

_____

Full-duplex Ethernet

_____

_____

Memory buffer

_____

_____

Microsegmentation

_____

_____

Propagation delay

_____

_____

Repeater

_____

_____

Segment

_____

_____

Sliding window

_____

_____

Switching

_____

_____

Focus Questions   **Name:** _____

Date: _____   **Class:** _____

1. Distinguish between cut-through and store-and-forward switching.

   _____
   _____
   _____

2. Describe full- and half-duplex Ethernet operation.

   _____
   _____
   _____

3. Describe the advantages of LAN segmentation that uses switches.

   _____
   _____
   _____

4. What are the differences between repeaters, hubs, bridges, switches, and routers?

   _____
   _____
   _____
   _____
   _____
   _____
   _____
   _____
   _____
   _____

5. What is a multiport repeater?

   _____
   _____

6. What is the difference between Shared Ethernet and Switched Ethernet?

   _____
   _____
   _____
   _____

7. Define the following terms:

Topology

_____

_____

VLAN (virtual LAN)

_____

_____

CCNA Exam Review Questions

The following questions help you review for the CCNA exam. Answers to these questions can be found in Appendix C, "Answers to the CCNA Exam Review Questions."

1. Which of the following broadcast methods does an Ethernet medium use to transmit and receive data to all nodes on the network?
    a. A packet
    b. A data frame
    c. A segment
    d. A byte at a time

2. What is the minimum time it takes Ethernet to transmit 1 byte?
    a. 100 ns
    b. 800 ns
    c. 51,200 ns
    d. 800 ms

3. Characteristics of microsegmentation include which of the following?
    a. Dedicated paths between sender and receiver hosts
    b. Multiple traffic paths within the switch
    c. All traffic visible on network segment at once
    d. a and b

4. LAN switches are considered to be which of the following?
    a. Multiport repeaters operating at Layer 1
    b. Multiport hubs operating at Layer 2
    c. Multiport routers operating at Layer 3
    d. Multiport bridges operating at Layer 2

5. Asymmetric switching is optimized for which of the following?
    a. Client/server network traffic where the "fast" switch port is connected to the server
    b. An even distribution of network traffic
    c. Switches without memory buffering
    d. a and b

6. In _____ switching, the switch checks the destination address and immediately begins forwarding the frame, and in _____ switching, the switch receives the complete frame before forwarding it.
    a. Store-and-forward; symmetric
    b. Cut-through; store-and-forward
    c. Store-and-forward; cut-through
    d. Memory buffering; cut-through

Engineering Journal (Continued)

Chapter 3   VLANs

Introduction

Chapter 2, "LAN Switching," discussed problems inherent in a LAN and possible solutions to improve LAN performance. You learned about the advantages and disadvantages of using bridges, switches, and routers for LAN segmentation and the effects of switching, bridging, and routing on network throughput. Finally, you briefly learned about the benefits of Fast Ethernet and *virtual local-area networks (VLANs)*. This chapter provides an introduction to VLANs and switched internetworking, compares traditional shared LAN configurations with switched LAN configurations, and discusses the benefits of using a switched VLAN architecture. When you finish the Chapter 3 online material and the print material in the *Cisco Networking Academy Program: Second-Year Companion Guide*, Second Edition, you should completely understand the following concepts.

Concept Questions

Demonstrate your knowledge of these concepts by answering the following questions in the space provided.

- An Ethernet switch is designed to physically segment a LAN into individual collision domains. **Do you understand how an Ethernet switch works? Explain.**
- VLAN technology is a cost-effective and efficient way of grouping network users into virtual workgroups, regardless of their physical location on the network. **Can you explain why?**
- VLANs work at Layer 2 and Layer 3 of the OSI reference model. **Can you explain why this is so?**
- Important to any VLAN architecture is the ability to transport VLAN information between interconnected switches and routers that reside on the corporate backbone. **Why is this so important?**
- The problems associated with shared LANs and switches are causing traditional LAN configurations to be replaced with switched VLAN networking configurations. **Why do VLAN configurations solve the shared LAN and switches problem?**
- The most common approaches for logically grouping users into distinct VLANs are frame filtering, tagging and frame identification. **Define frame filtering, tagging, and frame identification.**
- VLANs provide the following benefits:
  - They reduce administration costs related to solving problems associated with moves, additions, and changes. **How do VLANs reduce administration costs?**
  - They provide controlled broadcast activity. **What is controlled broadcast activity?**
  - They provide workgroup and network security. **How is this accomplished?**
  - They save money by using existing hubs. **Why are VLANs less expensive?**

Engineering Journal

In the space provided, answer the Concept Questions.

_____
_____
_____
_____
_____
_____
_____
_____
_____
_____
_____
_____
_____
_____
_____
_____
_____
_____
_____
_____
_____
_____
_____
_____
_____
_____
_____
_____
_____
_____
_____

Vocabulary Exercise Chapter 3   Name: _____

Date: _____   Class: _____

Define the following terms as completely as you can. Use the online Chapter 3 or the *Cisco Networking Academy Program: Second-Year Companion Guide*, Second Edition, material for help.

Access control list (ACL)

_____
_____
_____

Broadcast

_____
_____
_____

Broadcast domain

_____
_____
_____

Broadcast storm

_____
_____
_____

Collision domain

_____
_____
_____

Dynamic VLAN

_____
_____
_____

Firewall

_____
_____
_____

Flat network

_____

_____

_____

Frame

_____

_____

_____

Hub

_____

_____

_____

MAC (Media Access Control) address

_____

_____

_____

Microsegmentation

_____

_____

_____

Multicast

_____

_____

_____

Port

_____

_____

_____

Port-centric VLAN

_____

_____

_____

Focus Questions   **Name:** _____

Date: _____   **Class:** _____

1. What network problems might be caused if many LAN users change their location within a building over the course of a year?

    _____
    _____
    _____
    _____

2. Describe the benefits of VLANs.

    _____
    _____
    _____
    _____
    _____

3. What is the effect of VLANs on LAN broadcasts?

    _____
    _____
    _____
    _____

4. What are the three main VLAN implementations?

    _____
    _____
    _____

5. What is the purpose of VLAN frame tagging?

    _____
    _____
    _____
    _____

6. Define the following terms:

Static VLAN

    _____
    _____

VLAN

    _____
    _____

7. You are discussing installing a network for a customer. Outline the presentation you would give to the customer explaining VLANs and how you intend to put this technology to use in his/her application. Include a script of your opening and closing paragraph.

_____
_____
_____
_____
_____
_____
_____
_____
_____
_____
_____
_____
_____
_____
_____
_____
_____
_____
_____
_____
_____
_____
_____
_____
_____
_____
_____
_____
_____
_____
_____
_____
_____
_____
_____
_____
_____
_____
_____
_____

CCNA Exam Review Questions

The following questions help you review for the CCNA exam. Answers are found in Appendix C, "Answers to the CCNA Exam Review Questions."

1. The phrase *microsegmentation with scalability* means which of the following?
    a. The ability to increase networks without creating collisions domains
    b. The ability to put a huge number hosts on one switch
    c. The ability to broadcast to more nodes at once
    d. All of the above

2. Switches, as the core element of VLANs, provide the intelligence to do which of the following?
    a. They group users, ports, or logical addresses into a VLAN
    b. They make filtering and forwarding decisions
    c. They communicate with other switches and routers
    d. All of the above

3. Each _____ segment connected to a _____ port can be assigned to only one VLAN.
    a. Switch; hub
    b. Hub; router
    c. Hub; switch
    d. LAN; hub

4. Which of the following is *not* an advantage of using static VLANs?
    a. They are secure.
    b. They are easy to configure.
    c. They are easy to monitor.
    d. They automatically configure ports when new stations are added.

5. Which of the following is *not* a criterion on which VLANs can be based?
    a. Port ID and MAC address
    b. Protocol
    c. Application
    d. All of the above are criterion by which VLANs can be created

6. Which of the following is a beneficial effect of adding a VLAN?
    a. Switches do not need to be configured.
    b. Broadcasts can be controlled.
    c. Confidential data can be protected.
    d. Physical boundaries that prevent user groupings can be removed.

Engineering Journal (Continued)

Chapter 4   LAN Design

Introduction

One of the most critical steps to insure a fast and stable network is the design of the network. If a network is not designed properly, many unforeseen problems can arise and network growth can be jeopardized. The trend is toward increasingly complex environments involving multiple media, multiple protocols, and connection to networks outside a single organization's control. The design activity is truly an in-depth process, which includes the following:

- Gathering the user requirements and expectations
- Determining data traffic patterns, now and in the future, based on growth and server placements
- Defining all of the Layer 1, 2 and 3 devices, along with LAN and WAN topology
- Document the physical and logical network implementation

Washington Project

In this chapter, you begin the design phase of the Washington Project. The Washington Project is a real-world networking design problem. After you are employed in the networking field, you will face problems like this on a routine basis. The project takes you two semesters to complete, but you start working on the project in this chapter.

The project requires you to develop both LAN and WAN designs for a fictitious school district. Your class will most likely be divided into groups, and each group will be assigned a school complete with site layout plans. Each of your groups will develop an IP addressing scheme for the entire school district. Each group will present an IP addressing scheme and the class will agree on one implementation. One group will be elected as the Network Operations Center (NOC) contact that controls the distribution of all IP addresses.

Your long-term objective is to develop a LAN design for each individual school within the school district and then design a WAN that ties all the schools together. In each chapter of the *Engineering Journal and Workbook*, you are given an introduction to the portion of the case with which you deal. In the *Cisco Networking Academy Program: Second-Year Companion Guide*, Second Edition, you will find discussions and notes regarding the Washington Project. You want to work with the textbook and this journal to get the most from the project activity.

The result of your work should be documented in your Engineering Journal. We have provided space for your comments on the next page. You might also want to enter your thoughts in the Design Document in Appendix A, "Sample Design Document."

Engineeering Journal /Washington Project Deliverables
(The Washington Project requires you to accomplish certain tasks. These tasks that you
are asked to accomplish are known as deliverables. You are asked to "deliver" in this way
during the project and after you leave school and work in the industry.)

User Requirements Document for LAN Implementation
Get the user system requirements either from Appendix B or from your teacher and note
them here so that you will have a record of the requirements. You will refer to these
requirements often, so be sure to record them accurately and completely.

Network Growth Assumptions
LAN growth_____
WAN growth_____
Bits per second to any server host in the network_____
Bits per second to any host computer in the network_____
Level 3 and 4 protocols allowed_____
Two LANS one for _____ and the other for _____
LAN infrastructure will be based on _____
Describe the contents of the MDF.

_____
_____
_____
_____
_____

Describe the contents of the IDF room.

_____
_____
_____
_____
_____
_____

Each IDF will serve _____ workstations and will be supplied with
_____ runs for data.
Describe the configuration of each IDF Room.

_____
_____
_____

Submit overall design document, which will include:
Logical LAN design model of school
Complete physical design document including:
Detail of all MDFs/IDFs rooms including a to scale diagram.

_____
_____
_____

Quantity of HCC, VCC, and LAN Switch ports required to meet the existing and projected growth needs.

_____

Specifications on type and quantity of cable media for all horizontal and vertical runs.

_____

_____

Develop and document the IP addressing scheme for the district.

_____

_____

_____

Analyze network for positive and negative features.

_____

_____

_____

_____

_____

_____

_____

_____

_____

_____

_____

_____

_____

_____

Prepare and present to the class your overall district IP addressing scheme for consideration. (Work with the members of your group to develop an IP addressing scheme that you all feel will satisfy the system requirements. Be sure to consider all ideas and be thoughtful and collaborative as you determine the best alternative as a group.)

_____

_____

_____

_____

_____

_____

_____

_____

_____

_____

_____

_____

Vocabulary Exercise Chapter 4   Name: _____

Date: _____   Class: _____

Define the following terms as completely as you can. Use the online Chapter 4 or the
Cisco Networking Academy Program: Second-Year Companion Guide, Second Edition,
material for help.

Adaptability

_____

_____

Addressing

_____

_____

ARP

_____

_____

Availability

_____

_____

Backbone

_____

_____

Bandwidth

_____

_____

Broadcast domains

_____

_____

Broadcasts

_____

_____

Cable plant

_____

_____

Catchment areas

_____

_____

Coaxial cable

_____

_____

Collision detection

_____

_____

Collision domains

_____

_____

Contention

_____

_____

_____

_____

CSMA/CD

_____

_____

Design

_____

_____

Enterprise servers

_____

_____

Ethernet, 802.3

_____

_____

Ethernet switch

_____

_____

Extended star topology

_____

_____

Fast Ethernet

_____

_____

Firewalls

_____

_____

Functionality

_____

_____

Gigabit Ethernet

_____

_____

HCC

_____

_____

Host/ load requirements

_____

_____

IDF

_____

_____

Logical network

_____

_____

Manageability

_____

_____

MDF

_____

_____

Media

_____

_____

Microsegmentation

_____

_____

Migration

_____

_____

MIS throughput

_____

_____

Multicasts

_____

_____

Multimode fiber-optic

_____

_____

Network layer

_____

_____

Physical network

_____

_____

Physical network map

_____

_____

Port speed

_____

_____

Ports

_____

_____

Protocol

_____

_____

Routing table

_____

_____

Scalable internetworks

_____

_____

Scalability

_____

_____

Segmenting

_____

_____

Single-mode fiber-optic

_____

_____

Star topology

_____

_____

Subnets

_____

_____

Twisted-pair cable

_____

_____

VCC

_____

_____

Vertical cabling

_____

_____

WANs

_____

_____

Workgroup servers

_____

_____

10BaseT

_____

_____

100BaseFX

_____

_____

100BaseTX

_____

_____

1000 Base-LX

_____

_____

1000 Base-SX

_____

_____

1000 Base-T

_____

_____

CCNA Exam Review Questions

The following questions help you review for the CCNA exam. Answers are found in Appendix C, "Answers to the CCNA Exam Review Questions."

1. Which of the following is likely to cause congestion?
    a. Internet access
    b. Central database access
    c. Video and image transmission
    d. All of the above

2. Which of the following is *not* a cause of excessive broadcasts?
    a. Too many client packets looking for services
    b. Too many server packets announcing services
    c. Too many routing table updates
    d. Too many network segments

3. A primary data link-layer design goal is the selection of _____ devices, such as bridges or LAN switches, used to connect _____ media to form LAN segments.
    a. Layer 3; Layer 2
    b. Layer 1; Layer 2
    c. Layer 2; Layer 1
    d. Layer 2; Layer 3

4. Which of the following specifications for 10BaseT is wrong?
    a. Data rate = 10 Mbps
    b. Max length = 400 meters
    c. Signaling method = baseband
    d. Media = Category 5 UTP

5. Which of the following are benefits of implementing Layer 3 devices in your LAN:
    a. Allows segmentation of the LAN into unique physical and logical networks
    b. Filters data-link broadcasts and multicasts and allows for WAN connectivity
    c. Provide logical structure to the network
    d. All of the above

Engineering Journal (Continued)

Chapter 5   Interior Routing Gateway Protocol (IGRP)

Introduction

In Chapter 4, "LAN Design," you learned about LAN design goals and methodology. In addition, you learned about design considerations related to Layers 1, 2, and 3 of the Open System Interconnection (OSI) reference model. Reliability, connectivity, ease of use, ease of modification, and ease of implementation are other issues that need to be considered in building networks:

- To provide connectivity, a network must be able to incorporate a variety of hardware and software products in such a way that they can function together.
- To be easy to use, a network must perform in such a way that users need have no concern for or knowledge of the network's structure or implementation.
- To be easy to modify, a network must allow itself to evolve and adapt as needs change or expand, or as new technologies emerge.
- Finally, to be easy to implement, a network must follow industrywide networking standards, and it must allow for a variety of configurations that meet network users' needs.

In this chapter, you learn how the use of routers can help you address these issues. In addition, this chapter discusses how routers can be used to connect two or more networks, and how they are used to pass data packets between networks based on network protocol information. You also learn that a router can have more than one Internet Protocol (IP) address because it is attached to more than one network. An important function of routers is to examine incoming data packets and make path selections based on information stored in their routing tables. In this chapter, you learn more about how routers operate and what kinds of protocols they use. Finally, this chapter describes routing and IP routing protocols and discusses Cisco's proprietary implementation of Interior Routing Gateway Protocol (IGRP).

Washington Project: Configuring IGRP

In this chapter, you learn concepts and configuration processes that help you implement IGRP as the routing protocol in the Washington School District network. As part of the IGRP configuration and implementation, you need to complete the following tasks:

Engineering Journal/ Washington Project Deliverables

1. Identify and document the networks that will be advertised by the router located at the school district. Note this information here and in your design document.

----

2. Identify and document the IGRP AS number for the school district.

_____
_____
_____
_____
_____
_____

3. What is the router command sequence needed to implement IGRP on the school's router?

_____
_____
_____
_____
_____

4. How do routers ensure that the neighbor routers are aware of the status of all networks in the AS?

_____
_____
_____
_____
_____
_____

6. Identify the best settings for

Maximum hops _____

Holddown timer_____

Update timer_____

7. What are the appropriate bandwidth settings for serial interfaces?

_____
_____
_____

Vocabulary Exercise Chapter 5   **Name:** _____

Date: _____   **Class:** _____

Define the following terms as completely as you can. Use the online Chapter 5 or the
Cisco Networking Academy Program: Second-Year Companion Guide, Second Edition,
material for help.

AS (autonomous system)

_____

_____

Bandwidth

_____

_____

Convergence

_____

_____

Cost

_____

_____

Delay

_____

_____

Dynamic routing

_____

_____

Holddown

_____

_____

Hop

_____

_____

Hop count

_____

_____

IGRP (Interior Gateway Routing Protocol)

_____

_____

Interior protocol

_____

_____

Keepalive

_____

_____

Metric

_____

_____

MTU (maximum transmission unit)

_____

_____

Multiprotocol routing

_____

_____

Next-hop address

_____

_____

Path determination

_____

_____

Focus Questions

Name: _____

Date: _____   Class: _____

1. Path determination takes place at what layer of the OSI model?

_____

2. What is the layer function?

_____

3. How does a router determine on which interface to forward a data packet?

_____
_____

4. What does the term *multiprotocol routing* mean?

_____
_____

5. What are the two basic router factors that a dynamic routing protocol depends on?

_____

_____

6. What does the term *convergence* mean in network implementation?

_____
_____
_____

7. Describe the effects of a dynamic routing protocol, such as IGRP, on the performance and maintenance of the entire school district network.

_____
_____
_____

8. Your customer does not understand IGRP. How would you explain the concept of IGRP so that your customer can be better informed?

_____
_____
_____
_____
_____
_____
_____
_____
_____
_____
_____
_____
_____
_____
_____
_____
_____
_____
_____
_____
_____
_____
_____
_____
_____
_____
_____
_____
_____
_____
_____
_____
_____

CCNA Exam Review Questions

The following questions help you review for the CCNA exam. Answers are found in Appendix C, "Answers to the CCNA Exam Review Questions."

1. After a router determines which path to use for a packet, it can then proceed with which of the following?
    a. A broadcast
    b. Storing the packet in a routing table
    c. Choosing a routing protocol
    d. Switching the packet

2. The success of dynamic routing depends on which of the following?
    a. Manually entering routes
    b. Maintaining a routing table
    c. Periodic routing updates
    d. b and c

3. _____ routing protocols determine the direction and distance to any link in the internetwork; _____ routing protocols are also called shortest path first.
    a. Distance-vector; link-state
    b. Distance-vector; hybrid
    c. Link-state; distance-vector
    d. Dynamic; static

4. Which of the following is *not* a variable IGRP uses to determine a composite metric?
    a. Bandwidth
    b. Delay
    c. Load
    d. IGRP uses all of these

5. To select IGRP as a routing protocol, which command do you use?
    a. **show igrp**
    b. **router network igrp**
    c. **enable igrp**
    d. **router igrp**

Engineering Journal (Continued)

Chapter 6   Access Control Lists (ACLs)

Introduction

Network administrators face a dilemma: They must figure out how to deny unwanted access while allowing appropriate access. Although security tools such as passwords, callback equipment, and physical security devices are helpful, they often lack the flexibility of basic traffic filtering and the specific controls most administrators prefer. For example, a network administrator might want to allow users on the LAN to go out to the Internet through the LAN, but not want the users outside the LAN using the Internet to Telnet into the LAN.

Routers provide basic traffic filtering capabilities such as blocking Internet traffic, with access control lists (ACLs). In this chapter, you learn about using standard and extended ACLs as a means to control network traffic, and how ACLs are used as part of a security solution. An ACL is a sequential collection of permit or deny statements that apply to addresses or upper-layer protocols.

This chapter focuses on standard, extended, and named ACLs. In addition, this chapter includes tips, considerations, recommendations, and general guidelines for how to use ACLs, and includes the commands and configurations needed to create ACLs. Finally, this chapter provides examples of standard and extended ACLs and how to apply ACLs to router interfaces.

Washington Project

In this chapter, you learn the concepts and configuration commands that help you use and implement ACLs in the Washington School District network. In addition, as ACL concepts and commands are introduced, you can apply ACLs in your network design and implementation.

The LAN design for the Washington School District requires that each school have two networks: one for curriculum and the other for administration. Each unique LAN segment should be connected to a separate Ethernet port on the router to service that LAN. As part of the security solution, you need to devise an ACL for the router that will deny users from the curriculum LAN segment access to the administrative LAN segment, yet continue to give the administrative LAN users complete access to the curriculum LAN segment.

One exception to this ACL is that the router is to pass any Domain Name System (DNS) or e-mail traffic to the DNS/e-mail server, which is located on the administration LAN segment. This is traffic originating on the LAN that is accessed by the students. Therefore, if a student surfs the Web and needs the DNS server to resolve hostnames, this ACL will allow for hostname resolution. In addition, this ACL will allow students to send and receive e-mail.

When you use ACLs on the Washington School District routers, all traffic from the curriculum LANs should be prohibited on the administration LAN. You can make exceptions to this requirement by allowing applications such as e-mail and directory services to pass freely because they pose minimal risk.

E-mail and DNS need to be available throughout the district, and these types of services should not allow any unauthorized access to the administration network.

All the ACLs you create need to be controlled at the district office, and you need to review exceptions to the ACLs prior to implementation.

You need to develop a user ID and password policy for all computers attached to the Washington School District administration LAN. This policy should be published and strictly enforced.

Finally, you need make sure that all computers in the district network will have full access to the Internet.

The Internet connectivity you will need to implement in the Washington School District requires a double firewall implementation with all the applications that are exposed to the Internet, residing on a public backbone network. You need to ensure that all connections initiated from the Internet into each school's private network will be refused.

Engineering Journal/Washington Project Deliverables

1. Each school needs two networks, one for curriculum and one for administration. Draw the LAN design for each of these networks including separate Ethernet ports on the router.

2. Devise an ACL for the router that denies users from the curriculum LAN segment assess to the administrative LAN, yet give the administrative LAN users complete access to the curriculum LAN segment. Describe how you would proceed.

_____
_____
_____
_____
_____
_____
_____
_____
_____

3. How will you accommodate e-mail traffic and maintain security?

_____
_____
_____
_____
_____
_____

4. How will you develop a firewall for the two systems?

_____
_____
_____
_____
_____
_____
_____
_____

5. Develop the outline for the user ID and password policy.

_____
_____
_____
_____
_____
_____

6. How will you ensure that all computers on the network have Internet access and still maintain the level of security required?

_____
_____
_____
_____
_____
_____
_____
_____
_____

7. Outline in detail the security needs of this network.

_____
_____
_____
_____
_____
_____
_____

8. What is the purpose of ACLs?

_____
_____
_____

9. What condition does a standard ACL use for IP data packets?

_____
_____
_____

10. How do extended ACLs differ from standard ACLs?

_____
_____
_____
_____

11. How do ACLs compare each data packet to the conditions in the list?

_____
_____

12. How are standard and extended ACLs differentiated in the router?

_____
_____

Vocabulary Exercise Chapter 6   **Name:** _____

Date: _____   **Class:** _____

Define the following terms as completely as you can. Use the online Chapter 6 or the *Cisco Networking Academy Program: Second-Year Companion Guide*, Second Edition, material for help.

ACL (access control list)

_____

_____

Address filtering

_____

_____

Bit bucket

_____

_____

DDR

_____

_____

Deny

_____

_____

DNS (Domain Name System)

_____

_____

Extended access lists

_____

_____

Firewall

_____

_____

IP

_____

_____

Packet

_____

_____

Permit

_____

_____

Queuing

_____

_____

Standard access lists

_____

_____

TCP

_____

_____

TCP/IP

_____

UDP

_____

_____

Wildcard bits

_____

_____

Wildcard masking

_____

_____

CCNA Exam Review Questions

The following questions help you review for the CCNA exam. Answers are found in Appendix C, "Answers to the CCNA Exam Review Questions."

1. Which of the following commands would you use to find out whether there are any ACLs set on an interface?
   a. **show running-config**
   b. **show ip protocols**
   c. **show ip interface**
   d. **show ip network**

2. What do you call the additional 32 bits of information in the **access-list** statement?
   a. Wildcard bits
   b. Access bits
   c. Zero bits
   d. One bits

3. Using Router (config)# **access-list 156.1.0.0 0.0.255.255** is equivalent to saying which of the following?
   a. "Deny my network only"
   b. "Permit a specific host"
   c. "Permit my network only"
   d. "Deny a specific host"

4. When you issue a permit entry into an ACL that is accompanied by an implicit deny all, all traffic except that listed in the permit statement will be denied.
   a. True
   b. False

5. The **show access-lists** command is used to do which of the following?
   a. Monitor whether ACLs are set
   b. Monitor ACL statements
   c. Monitor ACL debugging
   d. Monitor groupings

Engineering Journal (Continued)

Chapter 7   Novell IPX

Introduction

Novell Netware is a network operating system (NOS), which connects PCs and other clients to NetWare servers. NetWare servers provide a variety of network services to their clients, including file sharing, printer sharing, directory services, and Internet access. Many NetWare servers function as application platforms for shared databases and as Internet and intranet servers. With more than 5 million networks and more than 50 million clients, Novell has the largest share of the NOS user base market.

In addition to Transmission Control Protocol/Internet Protocol (TCP/IP), Novell's Internetwork Packet Exchange (IPX) is another protocol that is commonly implemented in the networking industry. Until Novell's NetWare 5.0 release in 1998, all NetWare networks used IPX. As with AppleTalk, Novell has migrated NetWare to IP. Therefore, IPX networks must still be supported due to their installed base. In this chapter, you learn about Novell's IPX protocols, operation, and configuration.

Washington Project

In this chapter, you learn how to implement Novell's IPX in the Washington School District network. The school district needs a workgroup server in each of the computer labs at the school sites. The computer labs are located on the curriculum LAN segments of their respective sites. Both IP and IPX services need to be advertised across the school district network to other curriculum LAN segments.

When planning IPX addressing, you do not need to worry about numbering hosts as you would for TCP/IP. This is because the host address for a workstation is usually the MAC address of that station's network interface card (NIC). However, you need to develop a scheme for the IPX network numbers in the Washington School District WAN. *Remember:* A router cannot have two interfaces that belong to the same logical (IP, IPX, and so on) network, or subnet; therefore, you cannot use the same network number throughout the district WAN.

When you develop your IPX network numbering scheme, keep in mind that IPX network numbers can be up to 32 bits (or 8 hexadecimal digits), but they usually contain leading zeros to "pad out" the address. For example, the number 21 can be used as a valid IPX network number because leading zeros can be added to expand 21 into 32 bits (written as 8 hexadecimal digits): 00000021.

Some network administrators convert the IP network address to hexadecimal and use the result as the IPX network number. For example, the subnet 169.199.69.128 /27 would become A9C74580. But no rule says that you have to do this. You can use the leading zero feature to create simple IPX network numbers (such as 10, 20, 30, and so on).

You see later in this chapter that, because of Layer 2 issues, a router interface might need to exist on two logical networks; that is, have two network numbers simultaneously. After you read about Novell frame encapsulation types, you should check the Washington School District requirements carefully to see if your addressing scheme needs to account for this.

When configuring routers for the Washington School District, you should note what Novell servers are connected to a router's interface. If those servers are running NetWare 3.12 or 4.x, you must configure that interface to use Ethernet SNAP as a frame type. If you face a situation where two NetWare servers are connected to the same router port, and those servers use different frame types; you have to configure the router interface for multiple framing types. This means you must create multiple logical networks (that is, the interface will have two IPX addresses that have the same host number but different network numbers).

If a router's interface needs to exist on two different IPX networks to accommodate two different frame types or two different IP subnets, and if you run out of host space, you need to configure subinterfaces.

Engineering Journal/Deliverables

1. Draw the workgroup servers in each of the computer labs at the school sites. Which LAN are the workgroup servers located on?

2. Develop a scheme for the IPX numbers in the school district and document that scheme.

_____
_____
_____
_____
_____
_____

3. What are the two ways that you develop your numbering scheme?

_____
_____
_____

4. When two NetWare servers are connected to the same router port and use different frame types, what do you need to do to the router?

_____
_____
_____

5. What is connectionless protocol?

_____
_____
_____

6. Novell Netware uses_____ to facilitate the exchange of routing information and ____ to advertise network services.

7. The default encapsulation types on Cisco Router interfaces and their keywords are _____, _____, and _____.

8. Novell RIP is a distance vector routing protocol. What is a distance-vector routing protocol?

_____
_____
_____

9. What two metrics does Novell RIP use to make routing decisions?

_____

_____

10. What does GNS allow a client to do?

_____
_____
_____
_____

11. What does the term hop count refer to?

_____
_____

Engineering Journal (Continued)

Vocabulary Exercise Chapter 7   Name: _____

Date: _____   Class: _____

Define the following terms as completely as you can. Use the online Chapter 7 or the
Cisco Networking Academy Program: Second-Year Companion Guide, Second Edition,
material for help.

Cisco IOS (Internetwork Operating System)

_____
_____
_____

Client

_____
_____

Client/server

_____
_____

Enhanced IGRP (Enhanced Interior Gateway Routing Protocol)

_____
_____

Encapsulate

_____
_____

Frame

_____
_____

GNS (Get Nearest Server)

_____
_____

Hexadecimal (base 16)

_____
_____

IPX (Internetwork Packet Exchange)

_____
_____

MAC (Media Access Control)

_____
_____

NetWare

_____
_____

NLSP (NetWare Link Services Protocol)

_____
_____

NOS (network operating system)

_____
_____

Routing metric

_____
_____

SAP (Service Advertising Protocol)

_____
_____

Focus Questions Name: _____

Date: _____ Class: _____

1. In an IPX network, what is used for the host address?

   _____

2. What command do you use to set the maximum number of equal-cost paths the router uses when forwarding packets?

   _____
   _____

3. What command mode must the router be in before you can issue the **ipx routing** command?

   _____
   _____

4. What command do you issue to verify IPX address assignment on a router?

   _____
   _____

5. What command displays information about IPX SAP packets that are transmitted or received?

   _____

6. What is a routed protocol?

   _____
   _____
   _____

7. Are there any alternatives to IP?

   _____
   _____
   _____

CCNA Exam Review Questions

The following questions help you review for the CCNA exam. Answers are found in Appendix C, "Answers to the CCNA Exam Review Questions."

1. A Novell IPX address has 80 bits: 32 for the _____ and 48 for the _____.
   a. Network number; IP address
   b. Node number; MAC address
   c. Network number; node number
   d. MAC address; node number

2. When you configure an IPX network, you may need to specify an encapsulation type on which of the following?
   a. Just the Novell servers
   b. Just the Cisco routers
   c. Sometimes a and b
   d. Always a and b

3. Novell NetWare uses _____ to facilitate the exchange of routing information and _____ to advertise network services.
   a. NCP; RIP
   b. RIP; SAP
   c. SPX; NCP
   d. SAP; RIP

4. The syntax for configuring Novell IPX globally is which of the following?
   a. **ipx routing** [*node*]
   b. **router ipx**
   c. **ipx route** [*node*]
   d. **router rip**

5. Fill in the commands: _____ displays IPX status and parameters; _____ displays the contents of the IPX routing table; and _____ lists servers discovered through SAP advertisements.
   a. **show ipx traffic; show ipx route; show ipx routing activity**
   b. **show ipx interface; show ipx route; show ipx servers**
   c. **show ipx interface; show ipx; show ipx servers**
   d. **show ipx; show ipx route; show ipx**

Engineering Journal (Continued)

Chapter 8   Network Management

Introduction

Network Management contains many different areas. They include network documentation, network security, network maintenance, server administration, and server maintenance. This list is not all-inclusive, but it is more than enough to be covered at this time.

Each one of the listed topics is just as important as the rest, and none of them should be overlooked. The problem is that many administrators feel that, when the network is up and running, the job is over. This statement couldn't be further from the truth. When a network setup is complete, the real job of a network administrator starts.

Documentation

The first, and most critical, component for a good network is documentation. Documentation is the most talked-about and least performed task in a network. Documentation represents the network administrator's memory. The following documents assist you in properly documenting your network:

1. **Server and Workstation Configuration Details**

Computer Hardware Configuration Worksheet				
One Sheet Per Computer				
File Server or Workstation:				
Physical Location:				
Make and Model:				
Serial #:				
Company Invoice #:				
Removable Media Drives:				
Manufacturer	Drive Letter	Capacity	Internal/ External	Internal Drive Bay #
Fixed Media Drives:				
Manufacturer	Drive Letter	Capacity	Internal/ External	Internal Drive Bay #
Memory current/maximum:	Current:		Maximum:	

Peripheral Cards:						
Manufacturer		Model	Type	IRQ	DMA	Base Memory Addr.

Network Interface Cards:						
Manufacturer	Node Addr.	Model	LAN Driver	IRQ	DMA	Base Memory Addr.
Comments:						

Printer Configuration Worksheet One Sheet Per Printer						
Physical Location:						
Make and Model:						
Serial #:						
Company Invoice #:						
Printer ID #:						
Memory/current/maximum:	Current:			Maximum:		
Paper Bins	Bin #1 paper type		Bin #2 paper type		Bin #3 paper type	
Printer Configuration:						
Serial	Port	Baud Rate	Stop Bits	Parity	Xon/ Xoff	Interrupt
Parallel	Port	Polling				Interrupt
Network	IP Addr.	Polling	MAC Addr.			
Print Queues						
Print Operators:						
Comments:						

2. Software Listings

<table>
<tr><td colspan="6">Computer Software Configuration Worksheet
One Sheet Per Computer</td></tr>
<tr><td>Computer Invoice #:</td><td colspan="5"></td></tr>
<tr><td>Operating System(s)</td><td></td><td></td><td></td><td></td><td></td></tr>
<tr><td>Manufacturer</td><td>Version</td><td>Service Updates</td><td>Network Capable</td><td>Security</td><td></td></tr>
<tr><td></td><td></td><td></td><td></td><td></td><td></td></tr>
<tr><td></td><td></td><td></td><td></td><td></td><td></td></tr>
<tr><td>Application Software</td><td></td><td></td><td></td><td></td><td></td></tr>
<tr><td>Manufacturer</td><td>Version</td><td>Service Updates</td><td>Network Capable</td><td>Install Directory</td><td>Data Directory</td></tr>
<tr><td></td><td></td><td></td><td></td><td></td><td></td></tr>
<tr><td></td><td></td><td></td><td></td><td></td><td></td></tr>
<tr><td></td><td></td><td></td><td></td><td></td><td></td></tr>
<tr><td></td><td></td><td></td><td></td><td></td><td></td></tr>
<tr><td></td><td></td><td></td><td></td><td></td><td></td></tr>
<tr><td></td><td></td><td></td><td></td><td></td><td></td></tr>
<tr><td></td><td></td><td></td><td></td><td></td><td></td></tr>
</table>

3. Maintenance Records

<table>
<tr><td colspan="4">Computer Repair Worksheet
One Sheet Per Computer</td></tr>
<tr><td>Computer Invoice #:</td><td></td><td>Date:</td><td></td></tr>
<tr><td>Type of Problem:</td><td colspan="2">Hardware:</td><td>Software:</td></tr>
<tr><td>Problem Description:</td><td colspan="3"></td></tr>
<tr><td>Warranty Coverage:</td><td>Yes:</td><td>No:</td><td>Location of Repair:</td></tr>
<tr><td>Repair Description:</td><td colspan="3"></td></tr>
<tr><td>Department Charged:</td><td colspan="3"></td></tr>
<tr><td>Authorized By:</td><td colspan="3"></td></tr>
<tr><td>Repair Completed By:</td><td colspan="3"></td></tr>
<tr><td>Comments:</td><td colspan="3"></td></tr>
</table>

4. Security Measures

Network Security Room Form One Per Room					
Physical Location:				**Date:**	
Physical security:	Door Lock	Windows	False Ceiling	Fire Suppression	Locking Cabinets
Servers Tape Backup:					
Server Name:	Type	Media	Offsite Loc.	Tape Set Name	Start Day-of-Week
Server #1					
Server #2					
Server #3					
Authorized Access:	Name		Department		Function
Comments:					

Network Security User Form One Per User				
Physical Location:		**Date:**		
Username:		**User ID:**		
Department: **Password Length:**		Dept. Manager Home Dir:		
Date ID Expires:		Local Access:		
Access Hours:		Print Access:		
Remote Access:		Admin. Access:		
Inclusive groups:	Group name:	Group rights:	Local/Global	Restrictions
Network Duties/Privileges:				
Comments:				

Engineering Journal

Vocabulary Exercise Chapter 8   **Name:** _____

Date: _____   **Class:** _____

Define the following terms as completely as you can. Use the online Chapter 8 or the *Cisco Networking Academy Program: Second-Year Companion Guide*, Second Edition, material for help.

Cut sheet diagrams

_____
_____
_____

Data recovery

_____
_____
_____

Network access

_____
_____
_____

Back up operations

_____
_____
_____

Redundancy techniques

_____
_____
_____

Static, dust, dirt, and heat

_____
_____
_____

Power conditioning

_____
_____
_____

EMI

_____
_____
_____

RFI

_____
_____
_____

Software viruses

_____
_____
_____

Network baseline, updates, and change verification

_____
_____
_____

Peer-to-peer

_____
_____
_____

Client-server

_____
_____
_____

Network control

_____
_____
_____

Focus Questions

Name: _____

Date: _____

Class: _____

1. What types of network documentation are needed to properly manage a network?

_____
_____
_____
_____

2. Describe the benefits of network documentation.

_____
_____
_____
_____
_____

3. Describe the major components of network security related to network management.

_____
_____
_____
_____

4. What are the environmental factors that need be considered when managing a network?

_____
_____
_____

5. Describe the administrator's role in managing networks.

_____
_____
_____

6. Describe the scientific method for network troubleshooting.

_____
_____
_____
_____

7. You are discussing network management with a customer. Outline the presentation that you would give to the customer explaining network management and how you intend to manage his/her network. Include a script of your opening and closing paragraph.

CCNA Exam Review Questions

The following questions help you check your understanding of network management.
Answers are found in Appendix C, "Answers to the CCNA Exam Review Questions."

1. The type of backup that only saves the files that were modified on the same day as
   the backup operation is a
   - a. Full backup
   - b. Incremental backup
   - c. Copy backup
   - d. Differential backup

2. Raid 1 features what type of disk redundancy?
   - a. Disk striping
   - b. Disk backup
   - c. Disk duplexing
   - d. No redundancy

3. A network baseline is the comparison value to measure a network's
   - a. Security
   - b. Design
   - c. Structure
   - d. Performance

4. A peer to peer network establishes what type f relationship between end stations
   - a. Client to client
   - b. Client to server
   - c. Server to server
   - d. Server to Internet

5. Which type of file system does Windows NT use for security purposes?
   - a. Fat 16
   - b. Fat 32
   - c. NTFS
   - d. NFS

6. A document that shows the physical layout of a building's network wiring is
   called a
   - a. Cut sheet
   - b. Layout diagram
   - c. Floor plan
   - d. Access list

7. What is the minimum number of drives required for RAID 5?
   a. 1
   b. 2
   c. 3
   d. 4

8. In a client-sever network, the ability of a user to access certain files while not being able to access other files are the user
   a. Accesses
   b. Rights
   c. Abilities
   d. Securities

9. What is the IP address of the internal loopback?
   a. 10.10.10.1
   b. 255.255.255.0
   c. 127.0.0.1
   d. 192.0.0.1

10. A way to prevent static electricity damage is to
   a. Turn off the electricity when working on the computer.
   b. Wear rubber gloves to insulate the equipment.
   c. Use only plastic tools.
   d. Use a grounding strap.

Engineering Journal (Continued)

Chapter 9   WANs

Introduction

This chapter introduces the various protocols and technologies used in wide-area network (WAN) environments. You learn about the basics of WANs, including common WAN technologies, types of wide-area services, encapsulation formats, and link options. In this chapter, you also learn about point-to-point links, circuit switching, packet switching, virtual circuits, dialup services, and WAN devices.

Washington Project

The Washington School District WAN should connect all school and administrative offices with the district office for the purpose of delivering data. The information presented in this chapter helps you understand and design a district WAN that connects all the schools and administrative offices. In addition, you apply related concepts to the WAN design as you work through the chapter.

The WAN technology required for the Washington District network is a Frame Relay PVC. You should add the Frame Relay PVC to the Washington network design. In addition, you should implement a Frame Relay link to the Internet.

As part of the Washington School District network design and implementation, you need to determine what type of switches to obtain, how many of them to obtain, and where to place them in the network. Possible locations include the MDFs and IDFs in the school locations and at the main district office. Additionally, you need to determine what types of switches are needed, such as LAN or WAN switches, and whether they need to be Layer 2 or Layer 3 switches. Finally, you need to figure out the segmentation and security required in order to determine the types, number, and placement of switches in the network.

As part of the Washington School District network design and implementation, you need to determine what kind of CSU/DSUs to obtain, how many of them to obtain, and where to place them in the network. Possible locations include the MDFs in the school locations and at the main district office, where the WAN links will be terminated. Keep in mind that CSUs/DSUs need to be located close to routers.

Although both PPP and HDLC are appropriate frame types for point-to-point connections, you should use PPP on point-to-point links in the Washington School District network. PPP offers the following advantages:

- Interoperability between networking vendors

- LCP for negotiating basic line interoperability

- A family of network control protocols for negotiating individual Layer 3 protocols

The Washington School District should use dedicated lines for its WAN core. You need to determine how many links this will involve and what kinds of equipment must be purchased (such as CSUs/DSUs).

Engineering Journal Deliverables

1. Draw the school district WAN in diagram form.

2. You need to add Frame Relay PVC to your network design. How do you do that?

_____
_____
_____
_____
_____
_____
_____
_____

3. How do you establish a Frame Relay link to the Internet for the school district?

_____
_____
_____
_____
_____
_____

4. Identify the type and number of each type of switch that you will need.

Switch Type   Number

_____   _____

_____   _____
_____   _____
_____   _____
_____   _____

5. Using the drawing in Question 1, add the location of the switches that the network will require.

6. How many CSUs will your network require and where should they be placed?

_____
_____
_____
_____
_____
_____

7. How many DSUs will be required?

_____
_____
_____
_____

8. Why should you use PPP on point-to-point links in the network?

_____
_____
_____
_____
_____

9. Why not use HDLC as a frame type?

_____
_____
_____
_____
_____
_____
_____

Engineering Journal (Continued)

_____
_____
_____
_____
_____
_____
_____
_____
_____
_____
_____
_____
_____
_____

Vocabulary Exercise Chapter 9   **Name:** _____

Date: _____   **Class:** _____

Define the following terms as completely as you can. Use the online Chapter 9 or the *Cisco Networking Academy Program: Second-Year Companion Guide*, Second Edition, material for help.

ATM (Asynchronous Transfer Mode)

_____
_____

B channel (bearer channel)

_____
_____

Carrier network

_____
_____

Cisco IOS (Internetwork Operating System)

_____
_____

CO (central office)

_____
_____

CSU/DSU (channel service unit/digital service unit)

_____
_____

D channel (delta channel)

_____
_____

DCE (data circuit-terminating equipment)

_____

_____

DDR (dial-on-demand routing)

_____

_____

DLCI (data-link connection identifier)

_____

_____

DTE (data terminal equipment)

_____

_____

EIA (Electronic Industries Association)

_____

_____

Frame Relay

_____

_____

Hexadecimal (base 16)

_____

_____

LAPB (Link Access Procedure, Balanced)

_____

_____

Local loop

_____

_____

Modem (modulator-demodulator)

_____

_____

Partially meshed topology

_____

_____

PPP (point-to-point link)

_____

_____

POP (point of presence)

_____

_____

PVC (permanent virtual circuit)

_____

_____

Reliability

_____

_____

RBOC (regional Bell operating company)

_____

_____

SDLC (Synchronous Data Link Control)

_____

_____

SVC (switched virtual circuit)

_____

_____

TA (terminal adapter)

_____

_____

Toll network

_____

_____

Virtual circuit

_____

_____

WAN (wide-area network)

_____

_____

X.25

_____

_____

Focus Questions   Name: _____

Date: _____   Class: _____

1. Do a free-write on everything you learned about WANs. Include any terminology you have heard and what you know about it.

CCNA Exam Review Questions

The following questions help you review for the CCNA exam. Answers are found in Appendix C, "Answers to the CCNA Exam Review Questions."

1. How many data paths are used by WAN data-link protocols to frames to carry frames between systems?
   a. Two
   b. One
   c. Four
   d. Undetermined

2. At what layer of the OSI reference model would you find the DCE or DTE equipment?
   a. The network layer
   b. The data link layer
   c. The physical layer
   d. The transport layer

3. A CSU/DSU is generally used as what type of equipment?
   a. Router
   b. DTE
   c. Switch
   d. DCE

4. Which of the following encapsulation types are associated with synchronous serial lines?
   a. PPP
   b. HDLC
   c. Frame Relay
   d. All of the above

5. What encapsulation type would you select for a link if speed were the most important factor?
   a. Frame Relay
   b. PPP
   c. HDLC
   d. SLIP

6. Devices that are located at a service subscriber's site are referred to as what?
   a. Customer owned equipment
   b. Subscriber devices
   c. Customer premises equipment
   d. Subscriber premises equipment

7. The WAN path between DTEs is known as what?
   A. The link
   B. The circuit
   C. The channel
   D. All of the above

8. Which WAN services can be used with a router?
   A. Frame Relay
   B. ISDN
   C. PPP
   D. All of the above

9. Which of the following is an example of a packet-switched protocol?
   A. ISDN
   B. Frame Relay
   C. PPP
   D. HDLC

10. Which protocol does PPP use for establishing and maintaining point-to-point connections?
    A. HDLC
    B. LCP
    C. LAPD
    D. Cisco IETF

Chapter 10   WAN Design

Introduction

Today's network administrators must manage complex wide-area networks (WANs) in order to support the growing number of software applications that are built around Internet Protocol (IP) and the Web. These WANs require network resources and higher-performance networking technologies. WANs are complex environments involving multiple media, multiple protocols, and interconnection to other networks, such as the Internet. WANs need many protocols and features in order to permit growth and manageability.

Despite improvements in equipment performance and media capabilities, WAN design is becoming more difficult. Carefully designing WANs can reduce problems associated with a growing network environment. To design reliable, scalable WANs, network designers must keep in mind that each WAN has specific design requirements. This chapter provides an overview of the methodologies utilized to design WANs.

Washington Project

In this chapter, you learn about WAN design processes that will enable you to implement WAN services requirements into the Washington School District network design. The district WAN should connect all school and administrative offices with the district office for the purpose of delivering data.

First and foremost, you must understand your customers; in the case of the Washington School District, your customers include teachers, students, staff and administrators.

You need to determine whether the district has documented policies in place. You need to answer questions such as the following:

- Has district data been declared mission critical?

- Have district operations been declared mission critical?

- What protocols are allowed on the district network?

- Are only certain desktop hosts supported in the district?

Mission-critical data and operations are considered key to the business, and access to them is critical to the business running on a daily basis. You need to determine who in the district has authority over mission-critical data and operations, along with addressing, naming, topology design, and configuration. Some districts have a central Management Information System (MIS) department that controls everything. Some districts have small MIS departments and, therefore, must pass on authority to departments.

You need to find out what availability means to your customers, who in the Washington School District are teachers, students, administrators and staff. When analyzing your the district's technical requirements, estimate the traffic load caused by applications and by normal protocol behavior (for example, a new node joining the network). Estimate worst-case traffic load during the busiest times for users and during regularly scheduled network services, such as file server backups. This helps you understand what availability means to your customers.

Before you develop a district network structure and provisioning hardware, you need to determine the network traffic load that the district WAN needs to handle. You should determine all the sources of traffic and define what source characteristics must be ascertained. At this step, it is important to define the sources in sufficient detail that source traffic can be measured or estimated.

Additionally, you need to evaluate applications that might cause traffic problems in the Washington School District WAN. The following applications can generate large volumes of traffic and therefore can cause network problems, such as congestion:

- Internet access

- Computers loading software from a remote site

- Anything that transmits images or video

- Central database access

- Department file servers

The introduction of new sources or applications into the district WAN must be projected, along with likely growth rates. Obviously, this step requires considerable consultation with district end users and application developers. Finally, district network management data is an important source that you should not overlook because it might take up more than 15 percent of the total traffic volume.

Before you develop a district network structure and provisioning hardware, you need to determine the network traffic load that the district WAN needs to handle. You should determine all the sources of traffic and define what source characteristics must be ascertained. At this step, it is important to define the sources in sufficient detail so that source traffic can be measured or estimated.

The WAN core for the Washington School District network should be a high-speed switching backbone designed to switch packets as quickly as possible. School locations should connect into the WAN core based on proximity to the core from the school locations.

The Washington School District WAN should be based on a two-layer hierarchical model. Three regional hubs should be established one each at the district office, the service center, and Shaw Butte Elementary School in order to form a fast WAN core network.

You should provide access to the Internet or any other outside network connections through the Washington School District office by using a Frame Relay WAN link. For security purposes, no other connections should be permitted.

Engineering Journal/Deliverables

1. Who in the school district has authority over mission-critical data and operations? List the departments and individuals.

_____
_____
_____
_____

2. You will be serving many customers with this project. List the major network needs of your major customer groups.

Teachers

_____
_____
_____
_____

Students

_____
_____
_____

Staff

_____
_____
_____

Administrators

_____
_____
_____

3. Estimate normal and worst-case traffic load across the network.

_____
_____
_____
_____
_____

4. Where will the heaviest traffic be most likely to occur?

_____
_____
_____
_____
_____
_____
_____

5. Determine all sources of traffic and define what source characteristics must be identified.

_____
_____
_____
_____
_____
_____
_____
_____
_____
_____
_____

6. Internet access should be provided by using a Frame Relay WAN link. Why?

_____
_____
_____
_____

7. Draw a sketch of the WAN.

Vocabulary Exercise Chapter 10   Name: _____

Date: _____   **Class:** _____

Define the following terms as completely as you can. Use the online Chapter 10 or the *Cisco Networking Academy Program: Second-Year Companion Guide*, Second Edition, material for help.

Access layer

_____

_____

Circuit

_____

_____

Circuit switching

_____

_____

Core layer

_____

_____

Dedicated link

_____

_____

Distribution layer

_____

_____

Enterprise network

_____

_____

Frame Relay

_____
_____

Leased line

_____
_____

Link

_____
_____

Packet switching

_____
_____

T1

_____
_____

T3

_____
_____

WAN link

_____
_____

CCNA Exam Review Questions

The following questions help you review for the CCNA exam. Answers are found in Appendix C, "Answers to the CCNA Exam Review Questions."

1. Which of the following are initial concerns in a WAN design?
   a. Determining whether data outside the company is accessed
   b. Determining who is involved in the design from the customer standpoint
   c. Determining where shared data resides and who uses it
   d. All of the above

2. When analyzing network load requirements, you should check worst-case traffic load during what time of the day?
   a. The busiest time
   b. The least busiest time
   c. During network backups
   d. After regular work hours

3. When designing the WAN, where should application servers be placed?
   a. On the enterprise backbone
   b. Close to the users
   c. Near the point of presence
   d. Anyplace the designer chooses

4. Which of the following is not a benefit of a hierarchical design model?
   a. Scalability
   b. Ease of implementation
   c. A flat topology
   d. Ease of troubleshooting

5. In most cases, when designing the core layer, your main concern should be which of the following?
   a. Efficient use of bandwidth
   b. Workgroup access
   c. Server placement
   d. Enterprise server placement

6. Which of the following would be placed on the network backbone?
   a. Server
   b. Routers
   c. Workstations
   d. Application servers

7. Which layer connects users into the LAN?
   a. Workgroup
   b. Core
   c. Access
   d. Distribution

8. Which layer connects a LAN into a WAN link?
   a. Distribution
   b. Workgroup
   c. Core
   d. Access

9. In a one-layer design, the placement of what device becomes extremely important?
   a. Server
   b. Router
   c. Workstation
   d. Switch

10. In a two-layer design, what device would you use to segment the LAN into individual broadcast domains?
    a. Switches
    b. Routers
    c. Hubs
    d. Repeaters

Chapter 11   Point-to-Point Protocol (PPP)

Introduction

You studied wide-area network (WAN) technologies in Chapter 9, "WANs," and now it is important to understand that WAN connections are controlled by protocols that perform the same basic functions as Layer 2 LAN protocols, such as Ethernet. In a LAN environment, in order to move data between any two nodes or routers, a data path must be established, and flow control procedures must be in place to ensure delivery of data. This is also true in the WAN environment and is accomplished by using WAN protocols.

In this chapter, you learn about the basic components, processes, and operations that define Point-to-Point Protocol (PPP) communication. In addition, this chapter discusses the use of Link Control Protocol (LCP) and Network Control Program (NCP) frames in PPP. Finally, you learn how to configure and verify the configuration of PPP along with PPP authentication, and you learn to use Password Authentication Protocol (PAP) and Challenge Handshake Authentication Protocol (CHAP).

Washington Project

In Chapter 10, you learned about WAN design and developed the Washington School District's WAN design to allow connectivity between all sites in the district. Without a Layer 2 protocol, the physical WAN links have no mechanism to transmit data and implement flow control. In this chapter, you apply PPP as the data link-layer protocol to be used in the district WAN implementation.

Washington Project: PPP

In this chapter, you learn concepts and configuration processes that help you configure PPP in the Washington School District network. As part of the configuration, you need to complete the following tasks:

1. Apply PPP to the existing WAN designs.

2. Document the changes in the router configurations to implement PPP on the routers.

3. Document the router commands necessary to implement PPP on the router interfaces.

   - CHAP provides protection against playback attacks through the use of a variable challenge value that is unique and unpredictable.

   - Configure the interface for PPP encapsulation by using **encapsulation ppp**.

   - When PPP is configured, you can check its LCP and NCP states by using the **show interfaces** command.

Engineering Journal Deliverables

1. Discuss the difference between LCP and NCP.

_____
_____
_____
_____

2. What does the interface configuration look like for your WAN design?

_____
_____
_____
_____

3. Configure the interface for PPP encapsulation.

_____
_____
_____
_____

4. What changes in the router configuration must occur in order to implement PPP on the routers?

_____
_____
_____
_____

5. CHAP provides protection against playback attacks through the use of a variable challenge value. How and why does this work?

_____
_____
_____
_____
_____
_____
_____

Vocabulary Exercise Chapter 11   Name: _____

Date: _____   Class: _____

Define the following terms as completely as you can. Use the online Chapter 11 or the *Cisco Networking Academy Program: Second-Year Companion Guide*, Second Edition, material for help.

Apple Talk

_____

_____

Asynchronous physical media

_____

_____

Asynchronous serial

_____

_____

Authentication Phase

_____

_____

CHAP

_____

_____

Encapsulation

_____

_____

HDLC

_____

_____

LCP

_____

_____

Link Establishment

_____

_____

Link Establishment Phase

_____

_____

NCP (Network Control Progam)

_____

_____

Network layer protocol phase

_____

_____

Novell IPX

_____

_____

PAP

_____

_____

Physical media

_____

_____

PPP (Point-to-Point Protocol)

_____

_____

PPP Frame Format

_____

_____

SLIP (Serial Line Internet Protocol)

_____

_____

Synchronous

_____

_____

Synchronous circuits

_____

_____

Synchronous serial

_____

_____

TCP/IP

_____

_____

CCNA Exam Review Questions

The following questions help you review for the CCNA exam. Answers are found in Appendix C, "Answers to the CCNA Exam Review Questions."

1. Which of the following is the network-layer protocol supported by PPP?
   a. Novell IPX
   b. TCP/IP
   c. AppleTalk
   d. All of the above

2. In a PPP frame, what field identifies whether you have encapsulated IPX or TCP/IP?
   a. Flag
   b. Control
   c. Protocol
   d. FCS

3. When you're running PPP, LCP is responsible for which of the following?
   a. Establishment, maintenance, and termination of the point-to-point connection
   b. Maintenance of several links
   c. Router updates
   d. Compression

4. What type of handshaking occurs when PAP is the selected PPP authentication protocol?
   a. One-way
   b. Two-way
   c. Three-way
   d. Four-way

5. What command on the router can you use to check the LCP and NCP states for PPP?
   a. router> **show interfaces**
   b. router(config)# **show interfaces**
   c. router# **show interfaces**
   d. router(config-if)# **show interfaces**

Engineering Journal (Continued)

Chapter 12   Integrated Services Digital Network (ISDN)

Introduction

Many types of WAN technologies can be implemented to solve connectivity issues for users that need access to geographically distant locations. In Chapter 11, "Point-to-Point Protocol (PPP)," you learned about PPP. In this chapter, you learn about the services, standards, components, operation, and configuration of Integrated Services Digital Network (ISDN) communication. ISDN is specifically designed to solve the problems of small offices or dial-in users that need more bandwidth than traditional telephone dial-in services can provide; ISDN also provides backup links.

Telephone companies developed ISDN with the intention of creating a totally digital network. ISDN was developed to use the existing telephone wiring system, and it works much like a telephone. When you want to make a data call with ISDN, the WAN link is brought up for the duration of the call, and it is taken down when the call is completed; it's similar to how you call a friend on the phone, and hang up when you finish talking.

Washington Project

In this chapter, you learn the concepts and configuration process needed to implement an ISDN connection in the Washington School District WAN. You need to provide an ISDN connection for a remote site that needs part-time connectivity to the district.

You need to identify what additional equipment and media will be necessary in order to implement an ISDN link in Washington School District WAN design.

A small remote site will require connectivity to the Washington School District WAN from time to time. You should use ISDN technology to make the small site a remote node on the WAN.

Engineering Journal/Deliverables

1. What additional equipment will you need to establish an ISDN link for the WAN?

_____
_____
_____
_____
_____

2. What are the most common uses for ISDN?

_____
_____
_____
_____

3. Which type of ISDN service will you use for your project, BRI or PRI?
    What are the differences between the two?

_____
_____
_____
_____
_____
_____

4. What configuration process is needed to implement an ISDN connection?

_____
_____
_____
_____
_____
_____

5. What are the major advantages of an ISDN connection?

_____
_____
_____
_____
_____

Additional Thoughts:

_____
_____
_____
_____
_____

Vocabulary Exercise Chapter 12   **Name:** _____

Date: _____   **Class:** _____

Define the following terms as completely as you can. Use the online Chapter 12 or the *Cisco Networking Academy Program: Second-Year Companion Guide*, Second Edition, material for help.

2B+D

_____
_____

B channel (bearer channel)

_____
_____

BRI (Basic Rate Interface)

_____
_____

CO (central office)

_____
_____

CPE (customer premises equipment)

_____
_____

D channel (delta channel)

_____
_____

ISDN (Integrated Services Digital Network)

_____
_____

LAPB (Link Access Procedure, Balanced)

_____
_____

LAPD (Link Access Procedure on the D channel)

_____

_____

NT1 (network termination type 1)

_____

_____

NT2 (network termination type 2)

_____

_____

PBX (private branch exchange)

_____

_____

PRI (Primary Rate Interface)

_____

_____

Q.931

_____

_____

Reference point

_____

_____

Signaling

_____

_____

SOHO (small office/home office)

_____

_____

Focus Questions Name: _____

Date: _____ Class: _____

1. What is SPID (service profile identifier)?

_____
_____

2. What is TA (terminal adapter)?

_____
_____

3. What is TE1 (terminal equipment type 1)?

_____
_____

4. What is TE2 (terminal equipment type 2)?

_____
_____

5. What is UNI (User-Network Interface)?

_____
_____

6. What is the top speed at which ISDN operates?

_____
_____

7. How many B channels does ISDN use?

_____
_____

8. How many D channels does ISDN use?

_____
_____

9. The ISDN service provider must provide the phone number and what type of identification number?

_____

_____

10. Which channel does ISDN use for call setup?

_____

_____

11. The School Superintendent asks you to explain what ISDN is. She is not an experienced networker, but she is a competent manager. Develop an outline for explaining ISDN to her. Include your opening and closing paragraphs.

_____

_____

_____

_____

_____

_____

_____

_____

_____

_____

_____

_____

_____

_____

_____

_____

_____

_____

_____

_____

_____

_____

_____

_____

_____

_____

_____

CCNA Exam Review Questions

The following questions help you prepare for the CCNA exam. Answers are found in Appendix C, "Answers to the CCNA Exam Certification Review Questions."

1. At the central site, what device can be used to provide the connection for dial-up access?
    a. Switch
    b. Router
    c. Bridge
    d. Hub

2. For which of the following locations would ISDN service not be adequate?
    a. A large concentration of users at site
    b. A small office
    c. A single-user site
    d. None of the above

3. Protocols that begin with E are used to specify what?
    a. Telephone network standards
    b. Switching and signaling
    c. ISDN concepts
    d. It is not used with ISDN.

4. If you want to use CHAP for authentication when using ISDN, what protocol should you select?
    a. HDLC
    b. SLIP
    c. PPP
    d. PAP

5. On a router, which of the following commands do you use to set the ISDN switch type?
    a. Router> **isdn switch-type**
    b. Router# **isdn switch-type**
    c. Router(config-if)# **isdn switch-type**
    d. Router(config)# **isdn switch-type**

Engineering Journal (Continued)

Chapter 13   Frame Relay

Introduction

You learned about PPP in Chapter 11, "Point-to-Point Protocol (PPP)," and ISDN in Chapter 12, "Integrated Services Digital Network (ISDN)." You learned that PPP and ISDN are two types of WAN technologies that can be implemented to solve connectivity issues for locations that need access to geographically distant locations. In this chapter, you learn about another type of WAN technology, Frame Relay, that can be implemented to solve connectivity issues for users who need access to geographically distant locations.

In this chapter, you learn about Frame Relay services, standards, components, and operation. In addition, this chapter describes the configuration tasks for Frame Relay service, along with the commands for monitoring and maintaining a Frame Relay connection.

Washington Project

In this chapter, you learn the concepts and configuration procedures that enable you to add Frame Relay to the Washington School District network design. In addition, you learn the steps to implement a Frame Relay link to the Internet per the specification in the technical requirement document. This is the final step in your design and implementation of the district network.

In this chapter, you learn concepts and configuration processes that help you implement a Frame Relay data link in the Washington School District network. As part of the configuration and implementation, you need to complete the following tasks:

1. Document the insertion of Frame Relay in the WAN implementation, including:

    - DLCI numbers
    - The value of the CIR
    - A description of all data communication equipment needed to accomplish implementation

2. Document the router commands needed to implement Frame Relay on the router.

Engineering Journal/Deliverables

1. Identify all of the data communication equipment needed to accomplish the Frame Relay implementation.

_____
_____
_____
_____

_____
_____
_____
_____
_____

2. List the router commands needed to implement Frame Relay on the router.

_____
_____
_____
_____
_____
_____

3. Frame Relay WAN technology provides a flexible method of connecting LANs.
    Why is this so and how does it work?

_____
_____
_____
_____
_____
_____
_____
_____
_____

4. At this point, the entire Washington Project should be finished. What were the major
    problems that you encountered building this network?

_____
_____
_____
_____
_____

Vocabulary Exercise Chapter 13   **Name:** _____

Date: _____   **Class:** _____

Define the following terms as completely as you can. Use the online Chapter 13 or the *Cisco Networking Academy Program: Second-Year Companion Guide*, Second Edition, material for help.

BECN (backward explicit congestion notification)

_____

_____

CPE

_____

_____

DCE

_____

_____

DLCI (data-link connection identifier)

_____

_____

DTE

_____

_____

FECN (forward explicit congestion notification)

_____

_____

Frame Relay

_____

_____

Frame Relay Switch

_____

_____

LMI (Local Management Interface)

_____

_____

Local access rate

_____

_____

Media

_____

_____

PDN (public data network)

_____

_____

PVC (permanent virtual circuit)

_____

_____

Virtual circuit

_____

_____

Focus Questions   **Name:** _____

Date: _____   **Class:** _____

Describe the following:

Bc

_____
_____

BECN

_____
_____

CIR

_____
_____

DE

_____
_____

Excess Burst

_____
_____

FECN

_____
_____

Tc

_____
_____

CCNA Exam Review Questions

The following questions help you review for the CCNA exam. Answers found in Appendix C, "Answers to the CCNA Exam Review Questions."

1. How does Frame Relay handle multiple conversations on the same physical connection?
    a. It duplexes the conversations.
    b. It multiplexes the circuits.
    c. It converts it to an ATM cell.
    d. Multiple conversations are not allowed.

2. Which of the following protocols are used by Frame Relay for error correction?
    a. Physical and data-link protocols
    b. Upper-layer protocols
    c. Lower-layer protocols
    d. Frame Relay does not do error correction.

3. Which of the following does Frame Relay do to make its DLCIs global?
    a. It broadcasts them.
    b. It sends out unicasts.
    c. It sends out multicasts.
    d. DLCIs can't become global.

4. Which of the following is the data rate at which the Frame Relay switch agrees to transfer data?
    a. Committed information rate
    b. Data transfer rate
    c. Timing rate
    d. Baud rate

5. Which of the following assigns DLCI numbers?
    a. The end user
    b. The network root
    c. A DLCI server
    d. The service provider

6. DLCI information is included in which of the following fields of the Frame Relay header?
    a. The flag field
    b. The address field
    c. The data field
    d. The checksum field

7. Which of the following does Frame Relay use to keep PVCs active?
   a. Point-to-point connections
   b. Windows sockets
   c. Keepalives
   d. They become inactive.

8. How does Frame Relay use Inverse ARP requests?
   a. It maps IP addresses to MAC addresses.
   b. It maps MAC addresses to IP addresses.
   c. It maps MAC addresses to network addresses.
   d. It uses the IP address-to-DLCI mapping table.

9. Which of the following does Frame Relay use to determine the next hop?
   a. An ARP table
   b. A RIP routing table
   c. A Frame Relay map
   d. A IGRP routing table

10. For which of the following does Frame Relay use split horizon?
    a. To increase router updates
    b. To prevent routing loops
    c. To raise convergence times
    d. Frame Relay does not use split horizon.

Chapter 14   Network Management

Introduction

Now that you learned how to design and build networks, you can perform tasks such as selecting, installing, and testing cable, along with determining where wiring closets will be located. However, network design and implementation are only part of what you must know. You must also know how to maintain the network and keep it functioning at an acceptable level. In order to do this, you must know how to troubleshoot. In addition, you must know when it is necessary to expand or change the network's configuration in order to meet the changing demands placed on it. In this chapter, you begin to learn about managing a network by using techniques such as documenting, monitoring, and troubleshooting.

Vocabulary Exercise Chapter 14   Name: _____

Date: _____   Class: _____

Define the following terms as completely as you can. Use the online Chapter 14 or the *Cisco Networking Academy Program: Second-Year Companion Guide*, Second Edition, material for help.

Costs of a network

_____

_____

Error report documentation

_____

_____

Connection monitoring

_____

_____

Traffic monitoring

_____

_____

SNMP (Simple Network Management Protocol)

_____

_____

_____

RMON (Remote monitoring)

_____

_____

_____

Focus Questions   **Name:** _____

Date: _____   **Class:** _____

1. Why is the view of the network important?

_____
_____
_____
_____

2. Why is it necessary to monitor a network?

_____
_____
_____
_____
_____

3. Describe problem solving as it relates to network troubleshooting.

_____
_____
_____
_____

 4. Describe some troubleshooting methods.

_____
_____
_____

 5. Describe the administrative side of managing networks.

_____
_____
_____
_____

 6. Describe some software tools used for network troubleshooting.

_____
_____
_____
_____

7. You are discussing network management with a customer. Outline the presentation that you would give to the customer. Explain network management and how you intend to manage his/her network. Include a script of your opening and closing paragraph.

_____
_____
_____
_____
_____
_____
_____
_____
_____
_____
_____
_____
_____
_____
_____
_____
_____
_____
_____
_____
_____
_____
_____
_____
_____
_____
_____
_____
_____
_____
_____
_____
_____
_____
_____
_____
_____
_____

CCNA Exam Review Questions

The following questions help you check your understanding of network management. Answers are at found in Appendix C, "Answers to the CCNA Exam Review Questions."

1. Which protocol listed supports network management?
   a. SMTP
   b. NFS
   c. SNMP
   d. FTP
   e. IPX

2. To list your IP setting on a Windows NT computer, you would run the _____ command.
   a. IP
   b. IPCONFIG
   c. WINIPCFG
   d. SHOW IP
   e. CONFIG

3. One troubleshooting method used in network troubleshooting is
   a. Loopback readout
   b. Divide and conquer
   c. Ping of death test
   d. Trace the fault
   e. Reset the server

4. If the server is set up using the Internet Protocol, the clients must use which protocol to communicate with it?
   a. IPX
   b. UDP
   c. IP
   d. telnet
   e. HTTP

5. What is the most basic form of connection monitoring?
   a. WINIPCFG
   b. Tracert
   c. NetMonitor
   d. LanMeter
   e. Logging on

6. RMON is an extension of what protocol?
   a. SNMP
   b. UDP
   c. IPX
   d. PING
   e. SMTP

7. What does the **-n** protocol option stands for In the **ping** command?
    a. The network number of the ping area
    b. The no repeat option
    c. Count – number of pings
    d. Never stop until interrupted
    e. Nothing

8. How is the remote data gathered with RMON?
    a. Commands
    b. Tables
    c. Lists
    d. Probes
    e. User interaction

9. The cost of _____ equipment for mission-critical operations needs to be added to the cost of maintaining the network.
    a. Redundant
    b. Expensive
    c. Mechanical
    d. Security
    e. Welding

Engineering Journal

Network Design Definition

Design Definition

produced for

Organization

prepared by

Writer's Name

Department Name

Address of Organization

For internal use only

Table of Contents

Acknowledgments

On this page, acknowledge all persons who contributed to the contents of this document.

Purpose of this Document: To allow the networking administrator the ability to document creations, upgrades, and enhancements of the organization's network.

1. Project Scope

Use this section to document the scope of what you are designing. This section will include:

- An overview of what you are going to be designing.

- Purpose of why you are creating, upgrading, or enhancing a network.

- Organizations involved if you are creating a WAN and linking up with other organizations or enhancing your LAN to allow for other organizations to dial in to your WAN network.

1.1 Exercise 1
Please write your Project Scope in the space provided.

_____
_____
_____
_____
_____
_____
_____
_____
_____
_____
_____
_____
_____
_____
_____
_____
_____
_____
_____
_____
_____
_____
_____
_____
_____

2. Project Staffing Needs

- Title of individual that will be needed to support the network.
- Organization and Name of individuals who played a role in the network architecture.
- The role of the resource played.

2.1 Exercise 2

Enter in the network-design resources that have been working on the network design protect:

Resource Title	Contact Information	Role
	Organization: Name:	
	Organization: Name:	
	Organization: Name:	
	Organization: Name:	
	Organization: Name:	
	Organization: Name:	

3. Network Design Specifications

3.1 Local-Area Network and Wiring Closets

The local-area network design section has two sections: LAN topology and wiring closet configurations. Both of these sections contain a matrix. A matrix for network devices and a matrix for media used.

3.1.1 LAN Network Devices

This section includes an introduction to networking devices that are being used in the LAN. The introduction should detail the devices chosen based on your matrix analysis and why you chose those devices.

3.1.1.1 Exercise 3

Write the introduction to the Network Device section.

Introduction:

_____
_____
_____
_____
_____
_____
_____
_____
_____
_____
_____
_____
_____
_____
_____
_____
_____
_____
_____
_____
_____
_____
_____
_____
_____
_____
_____
_____

3.1.2 LAN Network Device Matrix
The section details why you decided on the devices mentioned in the introduction.

3.1.2.1 Exercise 4
Enter in your LAN network device matrix information. If you evaluated more than five products, use the products that are most relevant to the network architecture.

Network Decision Matrix

Specifications								

▼ Specifications Value ▼								
Alternatives								**TOTAL**

3.1.3 LAN Network Hardware/Software Profile

In the LAN design, what hardware and software configurations were decided on? In a typical LAN, distinctions are made among the various types of microcomputers as to their network function. For example, server microcomputers have resources, such as printers or disk drives, that are available for use by other microcomputers on the LAN. If you have a peer-to-peer network, each computer serves as a server, so detailed hardware/software profiles are not lengthy.

3.1.3.1   Exercise 5

Enter in the table all the hardware/software and protocol information for the LAN:

Hardware	Software	Protocol/Configuration	Location/Notes
Example: Cisco2501	Netware 3.x CiscoIOS	IPX,IP,NetBIOS,AppleTalk	Multiprotocal Router

3.1.4 LAN Wiring Closet

This section includes an introduction to wiring closets that are being used. The introduction should detail the different closets that are incorporated to talk to each other. In addition, this section contains the media overview and what media is used based on the media matrix.

3.1.4.1 Exercise 6

Write the introduction to the Wiring Closet section.

Introduction:

_____
_____
_____
_____
_____
_____
_____
_____
_____
_____
_____
_____
_____
_____
_____
_____
_____
_____
_____
_____
_____
_____
_____
_____
_____
_____
_____
_____
_____
_____
_____
_____
_____

3.1.5 LAN Wiring Closet Matrix
The section details why you decided on the media mentioned in the introduction.

3.1.5.1   Exercise 7
Enter in your media LAN matrix information. If you evaluated more than five media, use the connectors that are most relevant to the network architecture.

Network Decision Matrix

Specifications								

Alternatives	▼ Specifications Value ▼							TOTAL

3.1.6 LAN Wiring Closet Network Hardware/Software Profile

Depending on your topology (star, bus, ring) different cabling will be used. In addition, additional switches, routers, terminators, or microcomputers will be needed. In addition, network management software and protocols will be used. This section allows you to document the configurations in the wiring closet depending on your architecture.

3.1.6.1   Exercise 8

Enter in the table all the hardware/software and protocol information for the LAN:

Hardware	Software	Protocol/Configuration	Location/Notes
Example: Wiring Switch	CiscoIOS	Network Management software	Installed at South Park and Springfield closets.
Unshielded Twisted-Pair MAU	VINES NetBIOS	Attached to the AUI cable	

3.1.7 LAN Diagram

This section is for you to import your LAN diagrams from the ConfigMaker to MS Word.

3.1.8 LAN configuration Files

Insert all of your LAN configuration files from the hardware installed.

3.2 Wide-Area Network Services

3.2.1 WAN Network Devices
This section includes an introduction to networking devices that are being used in the WAN. The introduction should detail the devices chosen based on your matrix analysis and why you chose those devices.

3.2.1.1 Exercise 9
Write the introduction to the Network Device section.

Introduction:

_____
_____
_____
_____
_____
_____
_____
_____
_____
_____
_____
_____
_____
_____
_____
_____
_____
_____
_____
_____
_____
_____
_____
_____
_____
_____
_____
_____
_____
_____
_____
_____
_____

3.2.2 WAN Network Device Matrix

The section details why you decided on the devices mentioned in the WAN introduction.

3.2.2.1   Exercise 10

Enter in your WAN network device matrix information. If you evaluated more than five products, use the products that are most relevant to the network architecture.

Network Decision Matrix

	Specifications								
	▼ Specifications Value ▼								
Alternatives									**TOTAL**

3.2.3 WAN Network Devices Hardware/Software Profile

In the WAN design what hardware and software configurations were decided on? Generally, wide-area network is a general term referring to all networks that cover a broad area because of various nodes or stations that are geographically separated by long distances. These stations serve as gateways to other locations.

3.2.3.1   Exercise 11

Enter in the table all the hardware/software and protocol information for the WAN:

Hardware	Software	Protocol/Configuration	Location/Notes
Southpark WAN server	WAN Network Manager CiscoIOS	Packet Assembly/Disassembly	

3.2.4 WAN Network Media and Service
This section includes an introduction to wiring closets that are being used. The introduction should detail the different closets that are incorporated to talk to each other. In addition, this section contains the media overview and what media is used based on the media matrix.

3.2.4.1   Exercise 12
Write the introduction to the WAN media and services section.

Introduction:

_____

_____

_____

_____

_____

_____

_____

_____

_____

_____

_____

_____

_____

_____

_____

_____

_____

_____

_____

_____

_____

_____

_____

_____

_____

_____

_____

_____

_____

_____

_____

_____

_____

_____

_____

_____

_____

_____

3.2.5 WAN Network Media and Service Matrix
This section details why you decided on the media, service, or devices mentioned in the introduction.

3.2.5.1   Exercise 13
Enter in your media WAN matrix information. If you evaluated more than five media, use the connectors that are most relevant to the network architecture.

Network Decision Matrix

Specifications								

Alternatives	Specifications Value								TOTAL

3.2.6 WAN Network Media and Service Hardware/Software Profile

A typical WAN transmits data over public thoroughfares, roads, and streets, and, therefore, must use the communication circuits of a publicly registered common carrier (Sprint, AT&T, and MCI). In this section, you can identify any communication circuits in the hardware sections.

3.2.6.1   Exercise 14

Enter in the table all the hardware/software and protocol information for the WAN:

Hardware	Software	Protocol/Configuration	Location/Notes
Southpark WAN server	WAN Network Manager CiscoIOS	Packet Assembly/Disassembly	

3.2.7 WAN Diagram

This section is for you to import your WAN diagrams from the ConfigMaker to MS Word.

3.2.8 WAN Configuration Files

Insert all of your WAN configuration files from the hardware installed.

3.2.9 Domain Name Service and E-Mail
Identify all DNS and E-mail configurations that were set up for LAN/WAN communication during integration. Will there be DNS servers? If so, where will they be located? Who will be administering the servers?

3.2.9.1 Exercise 15
Give a brief overview of the processes and procedures that you performed on the LAN/WAN configurations:

_____

_____

_____

_____

_____

_____

_____

_____

_____

_____

_____

3.2.10 Server Implementation
Of the servers that were donated to the LAN/WAN network, which ones are in the WAN configuration?

3.2.10.1 Exercise 16
Identify the donated servers that were put into the LAN/WAN:

Machine Type	Machine Location	Configuration (LAN/WAN?)

3.2.11 Security Access
Within a LAN/WAN, there are certain security procedures a networking administrator can put in place to protect an organization. Will the security be hardware? Will the security be based on an access list? Will the district have different security than local schools?

3.2.11.1 Exercise 17
Give a brief description of security that a LAN/WAN would need within your case study.

_____

_____

_____

_____

_____

3.2.12 LAN and WAN Addressing Network Management

How does a network administrator set up IP addressing for the LAN and WAN communication? Will some machines need static IP addressing and others need dynamic IP addressing? Who will be administering the network? How will they be able to access the network? What standards will be used and how will the hardware be recognized on the network?

3.2.12.1 Exercise 18

Give a summary of how the LAN/WAN will be configured:

_____

_____

_____

_____

_____

_____

_____

_____

_____

_____

_____

_____

_____

_____

_____

_____

_____

_____

_____

_____

_____

_____

_____

_____

_____

_____

_____

_____

_____

_____

_____

_____

_____

_____

_____

4. Technical Support Plan

- Title of individual that will be needed to support the network.
- Organization and name of individuals who play a daily, weekly, monthly role
- What do each of these individuals do to support the ongoing support

4.1.1.1   Exercise 19

Enter in the network design resources that have been working on the network design project. Make sure that you have a duty pager or someone that gets paged when the network goes down.

Resource Title	Contact Information	Role
	Organization: Name:	
	Organization: Name:	
	Organization: Name:	
	Organization: Name:	
	Organization: Name:	
	Organization: Name:	

Appendix B   Washington Project Background

Objective

The purpose of the Threaded Case Study (TCS) is to engage the students in learning by allowing them to apply the knowledge that they have gained to a real-life example.

Overview of Threaded Case Study

The TCS is a performance assessment that is introduced in the first semester, although the actual project work will not be done until the third and fourth semesters. As concepts are introduced, students learn to apply them. The *Engineering Journal* and the Study Guide contain content, concepts, and understandings from the first two semesters that will assist in building the prerequisite knowledge for the TCS. A large school district in Phoenix, Arizona, will be the field model that is included in the TCS.

Each team of students will be given architectural drawings (electronically) of the various schools along with the actual wiring drawings (electronic format.). The completed design considerations and specifications document will be included as a teacher resource. Each student will keep an engineering journal and a Study Guide during the four-semester course. Teams of students will submit a final design document and make an oral presentation of their project near the end of the fourth semester. Criteria for the project will be a series of rubrics that are linked to National Standards in the areas of Science, Mathematics, Reading, Writing, and SCANS.

Technology Implementation Requirements

General Requirements

The school district is in the process of implementing a enterprise wide network which will include local-area networks (LANs) at each site and a wide-area network (WAN) to provide data connectivity between all school sites.

Access to the Internet from any site in the school district is also an integral part of this implementation. After the network is in place, the school district will implement a series of servers to facilitate online automation of all of the districts administrative and many of the curricular functions.

Because this network implementation must continue to be functional for a minimum of 7-10 years, all design considerations should include 100 percent growth in the LANs and 100 percent growth in the WAN. The minimum requirement for initial implementation design will be 1.0 Mega Bits per second to any host computer in the network and 100 Mbps to any server host in the network. Only two OSI Layer 3 and 4 protocols will be allowed to be implemented in this network, they are TCP/IP and Novell's IPX.

TABLE OF CONTENTS

SECTION 1 – Wide-Area Network

The Washington School District WAN will connect all school and administrative offices with the district office for the purpose of delivering data. The WAN will be based on a two layer hierarchical model. Three regional hubs will be established at the District Office, Service Center and Shaw Butte Elementary School for the purpose of forming a fast WAN core network. School locations will be connected into the WAN core hub locations based on proximity to hub.

TCP/IP and Novell IPX will be the only networking protocols that will be acceptable to traverse the district WAN. All other protocols will be filtered at the individual school sites using Routers. Routers will also be installed at each WAN core location. Access to the Internet or any other outside network connections will be provided through the District Office through a frame relay WAN link. For security purposes, no other connections will be permitted.

SECTION 2 – Local-Area Network and Wiring Scheme

Two LAN segments will be implemented in each school and the District office. The transport speeds will be Ethernet 10BaseT, 100BaseT, and 100baseFx. Horizontal cabling shall be Category 5 Unshielded Twisted-Pair (CAT5 UTP) and will have the capacity to accommodate 100 mbps. Vertical (Backbone) cabling shall be CAT5 UTP or fiber-optic multimode cable. The cabling infrastructure shall comply with EIA/TIA 568 standards.

One LAN will be designated for student / curriculum usage and the other will be designated for administration usage (see Section 5, "Security"). The LAN infrastructure will be based on Ethernet LAN switching that will allow for a migration to faster speeds (more bandwidth) to the individual computers and between MDFs and IDFs without revamping the physical wiring scheme to accommodate future applications.

In each location, a Main Distribution Facility (MDF) room will be established as the central point to which all LAN cabling will be terminated and will also be the point of presence for the WAN connection. All major electronic components for the network, such as the routers and LAN switches will be housed in this location. In some cases, an Intermediate Distribution Facility (IDF) room will be established, where horizontal cabling lengths exceed EIA/TIA recommended distances or where site conditions dictate. In such cases, the IDF will service its geographical area and the IDF will be connected directly to the MDF in a star or extended star topology.

Each room requiring a connection to the network will be able to support 24 workstations and be supplied with 4 CAT 5 UTP runs for data, with 1 run terminated at the teachers workstation. These cable runs will be terminated in the closest MDF or IDF. All CAT 5 UTP cable runs will be tested end-to-end for 100 mbps bandwidth capacity. A single location in each room will be designated as the wiring point of presence (POP) for that room. It will consist of a lockable cabinet containing all cable terminations and electronic components; that is, data hubs. From this location, data services will be distributed within the room via decorative wire molding. Network 1 will be allocated for general curriculum usage and network 2 will allocated for administrative usage.

SECTION 3 – District Supplied Servers and Functions

All file servers will be categorized as Enterprise or Workgroup type services and then placed on the network topology according to function and anticipated traffic patterns of users.

Domain Names and E-Mail Services

Domain Name Services (DNS) and e-mail delivery will be implemented in a hierarchical fashion with all services located on the master server at the district office. Each hub location will contain a DNS server to support the individual schools serviced out of that location. Each school will also contain a host for DNS and e-mail services (local post office) that will maintain a complete directory of all staff personnel and student population for that location. The school host will be the local post office box and will store all e-mail messages. The update DNS process will flow from the individual school server to the hub server and to the district server. All regional servers will have the capability to communicate between themselves thus building redundancy in the system in the event that the District master server is unavailable. Should the District master server require a partial or complete restore of data, the ability to query any or all of the regional servers to acquire the needed information would be provided.

Administrative Server

The school district is moving towards a totally automated server based administration system. Each school location will contain an administration server, which will house the student tracking, attendance, grading, and other administration functions. This server will be running TCP/IP as its OSI Layer 3 and 4 protocols and will only be made available to teachers and staff.

Library Server

The school district is implementing an automated library information and retrieval system, which will house an online library for curricular research purposes. This server will be running TCP/IP as its OSI Layer 3 and 4 protocols and will made available to anyone at the school site.

Application Server

All computer applications will be housed in a central server at each school location. As applications, such as Word, Excel, PowerPoint, and so on, are requested by users, these applications will be retrieved from the application server. This will provide district support staff with an easy and efficient method for upgrading applications without having to reload new software on each computer in the district network. This server will use TCP/IP as its OSI Layer 3 and 4 protocols and will be made available to anyone at the school site.

Other Servers

Any other servers implemented at the school sites will be considered departmental (workgroup) servers and will be placed according to user group access needs. Prior to implementation of other servers a requirements analysis must be submitted for the purpose of determining placement of the server on the district network.

SECTION 4 – Addressing and Network Management

A complete TCP/IP addressing and naming convention scheme for all host, servers, and network interconnect devices will be developed and administered by the District Office. The implementation of unauthorized addresses will be prohibited. All computers located on the administrative networks will have a static address; curriculum computers will obtain addresses by utilizing Dynamic Host Configuration Protocol (DHCP).

A master network management host will be established at the District Office and will have total management rights over all devices in the network. This host will also serve as the router configuration host and maintain the current configurations of all routers in the network. Each region location will house a regional network management host to support its area. The management scheme for the data portion of the network will be based on the Simple Network Management Protocol (SNMP) standards. All routers will be pointed to the master Network Management host for the purpose of downloading new or existing configurations. The District Office will maintain the super user passwords for all network devices and configuration changes on these devices will be authorized from the District Office (i.e., routers and LAN switches).

SECTION 5 - Security

External Threats - Internet Connectivity shall utilize a double firewall implementation with all Internet exposed applications residing on a public backbone network. In this implementation all connections initiated from the Internet into the schools private network will be refused. In the district security model, the network will be divided into three logical network classifications: administrative, curriculum, and external with secured interconnections between them.

This model will dictate that two physical LAN infrastructures be installed at all schools and the District Office, with one designated administrative and the other curriculum. Every computer and file server will be categorized according to its function and placed on the appropriate LAN segment. At the schools each LAN segment will have a file server. All applications will be categorized and placed on the appropriate server.

By utilizing access control lists (ACLs) on the routers, all traffic from the curriculum LANs will be prohibited on the administration LAN. Exceptions to this ACL can be made on an individual basis. Applications such as e-mail and directory services will be allowed to pass freely since they pose no risk.

A user ID and Password Policy will be published and strictly enforced on all computers attached to the administration LAN. All computers in the District network will have full access to the Internet.

All ACLs will be controlled at the District Office and exceptions to the ACLs will be reviewed prior to implementation.

SECTION 6 – Internet Connectivity

All Internet connectivity will be supplied through the District Office with the District Office being the single point of contact for all schools and organizations within the district. This connection will be highly controlled and capacity (bandwidth) upgraded as usage dictates.

Internet connection will utilize double firewall implementation with a public network (Ethernet backbone) established for services that will be exposed to the Internet such as master e-mail, Domain Name Services (DNS), and a World Wide Web server.

All connectivity that is initiated from the Internet to the internal District network will be protected via Access Control Lists (ACLs) on the routers that make up the double firewall architecture. Any connectivity initiated from the District to the Internet will be permitted to communicate freely. E-mail and DNS services will communicate freely in both directions since these applications poses no security threat.

A Web server will be located on the public backbone and partitioned to allow any school to install a Web home page on the Internet. Individual Web servers that need total exposure to the Internet will not be permitted on the internal district network. If schools require an independent, Web-server host, this host will be placed on the public network backbone.

Appendix C

Answers to the CCNA Exam Review Questions

Chapter 1
1. a
2. e
3. d
4. e
5. c

Chapter 2
1. b
2. b
3. d
4. d
5. a
6. b
7. d

Chapter 3
1. a
2. d
3. c
4. d
5. d
6. a

Chapter 4
1. d
2. d
3. c
4. b
5. d

Chapter 5
1. d
2. d
3. a
4. d
5. d

Chapter 6
1. c
2. a

3. c
4. a
5. b

Chapter 7
1. c
2. d
3. b
4. a
5. b

Chapter 8
1. b
2. c
3. d
4. a
5. c
6. a
7. c
8. b
9. c
10. d

Chapter 9
1. b
2. c
3. d
4. d
5. a
6. c
7. d
8. d
9. b
10. b

Chapter 10
1. d
2. a
3. b
4. c
5. a

6. b
7. c
8. d
9. a
10. b

Chapter 11
1. d
2. c
3. a
4. b
5. c

Chapter 12
1. b
2. a
3. a
4. c
5. d

Chapter 13
1. b
2. b
3. c
4. a
5. d
6. b
7. c
8. d
9. c
10. b

Chapter 14
1. c
2. b
3. b
4. c
5. e
6. a
7. c
8. d
9. a

Notes